To

Jean,

Wishing you the

Fred Gottlieb

28/9/99

BATTLEFIELDS OF LIFE

BATTLEFIELDS OF LIFE

Fred Goddard

The Book Guild Ltd
Sussex, England

The Book Guild Ltd
25 High Street,
Lewes, Sussex

First published 1999
© Fred Goddard, 1999
Set in Times
Typesetting by Keyboard Services, Luton

Printed in Great Britain by
Bookcraft Ltd (Bath), Avon

A catalogue record for this book is
available from the British Library

ISBN 1 85776 426 9

This book is dedicated to my late wife Doris Rose Goddard, who passed away 8 January 1997. Doris was all that could be wished for as a loving wife and devoted mother to our four children. Sadly missed by myself, Valerie, Raymond, Dennis and Richard.

CONTENTS

ACKNOWLEDGEMENTS

Many thanks to the following:

The first proofs were read by Brian Giltrow, a friend from our wine club, who lives in Lindfield. I have received from him endless assistance and advice throughout, and it is largely due to him that the book does not contain innumerable errors and mistakes.

I thank Linda Helliwell for her invaluable help with subsequent proofs: mainly for her swift and accurate typing of the manuscript, done entirely in her own time.

Many thanks to Vic Haydon and his wife, Edna, for their kind help with advice, part-editing, and helpful criticisms. Also for Vic's help during my battle with the War Pension Department.

I cannot thank enough Michael Denman, who owns the photographic shop in the Broadway, Haywards Heath, for his highly professional work in bringing some of my old photos back to life. I'm sure when I kept walking into the shop he must have been saying under his breath, 'Oh God, not him again!' Many thanks, Michael.

Bridget – how can I thank her enough for putting up with me in Northern Ireland over what must be the last thirty years? It was during one of my many visits to Michael and Bridget Winter's home that this book was born and Bridget eventually carried out some part-editing. Thanks, Bridget.

To Nicholas Soames MP, for taking up so much of his valuable time reading my humble manuscript and his subsequent written comments, for which I am very grateful.

Last but not least, the family's old friend, Paddy Henry, who was the first one to pressure me into writing this book. Paddy's help through his many friends has been invaluable. I raise my glass, as I have done so many times before – 'Cheers, Paddy'.

FOREWORD

I am honoured to be invited to write a foreword to Fred
Goddard's book. It is the most splendid work and Fred deserves
great congratulations for having taken the trouble, time and
effort to put together such a fascinating and remarkable story.

This is a piece of real contemporary history and the story of
a man of great character, determination and courage.

All who read it will derive great pleasure from it and further-
more will learn of the great efforts and sacrifices of ordinary
people in war time, as well as their everyday stuggles in peace.

Nicholas Soames

PREFACE

Let us then be up and doing
With a heart for any fate
Still achieving, still pursuing
Learn to labour and to wait

H. W. Longfellow

This is the story of Fred Goddard of Bentswood Road, Haywards Heath. Fred is now in his eighties and remarkably tough and resilient. Before this book, he had never written anything in his life, and at first glance he appears to be an average elderly gentleman who has led a fairly comfortable life, worked as a plumber and, along with his late wife Doris, provided for and brought up their family of four children.

First glances can be very deceptive, and never was this more true than in Fred's case. On occasions Fred had told me about parts of his life, particularly his early years, his experiences in the war and his working life. I found them so fascinating and riveting that I prevailed upon him with others to write his lifestory.

Fred has written his story and tells it with modesty and with no attempt at dramatics, yet he emerges as a man of great moral and physical courage. He has remarkable optimism and compassion; the only sad aspect is that his beloved wife Doris is not alive to read it, but I am sure that she is shaking her head and smiling because she was the great support in his life and still is his inspiration.

In my opinion this book provides a great insight into the hardship and dangers that ordinary people encountered at the turn of the last century and during the wars and after, but above all else it portrays an incredible determination and optimism to get on with life and play the hand you are dealt without whingeing. It is a valuable contribution to understanding the life and times of that period, and Fred is to be congratulated for placing it before the public.

Paddy Henry
Haywards Heath, November 1998

INTRODUCTION

This book was written in manuscript in 1998. It was originally suggested that I should write it by a very long-standing friend of the family, Paddy Henry. At first I declined, believing my limited education would not be up to a standard to achieve such a task. My impression had always been that authors must be very educated people. The two things which worried me were my grammar and spelling. It so happened that I was talking to another friend, Brian Giltrow, one evening and he, being very interested in stories of the war years, asked about my service history. After telling him a little about it, Brian suggested I should write a book. I had been told that Brian had, at one time, been connected with publishing. After telling him that another friend had also suggested the same thing but also about my worries, it was Brian who told me that many authors suffer from the same anxieties about their work. He thought it was a shame that stories like mine would never be known. For some time I turned the thought over in my mind, and the next time I met Brian I asked him if he would help by checking my spelling, etc. This he agreed to do. I then approached Linda Helliwell, who is our secretary, to type out the manuscript for me and make a little 'fine tuning', so allowances must be made, this is after all my own story.

1

Broken School Days

My early life was something of a mystery. According to records, I was born in Cuckfield Hospital in West Sussex, on 15 December 1916, to Percy and Olive Goddard of Haywards Heath. For some unaccountable reason, the first memories of my life were of my foster parents Mr and Mrs Beil, who lived in Wivelsfield, a little way from what is now called Valebridge Road. I recall that they were Americans, extremely nice people, and I had a happy upbringing with a foster brother named Sid.

Sid was about the same age as myself, and we went to the Junction Road primary school. Our foster parents had a very large holding stretching down into Jane's Lane and out over Valebridge Road to the London and Brighton railway bank. I remember that we used to go haymaking in the fields under the railway bank, where I used to love the smell of the smoke from the steam trains when they passed by. Today those fields are bungalow sites. We had cows, sheep and goats on the land.

I must point out at this stage that, although I have been referring to Mr and Mrs Beil as my foster parents, I have never been able to find out the true arrangements between my real parents and the Beils. All I can say for certain is that no legal arrangements had been made. I always suspected that the Beils were unable to have children.

I do not know to this day why I was fostered out, but my life suddenly changed on a Saturday summer's morning in 1924 when a young man arrived to take me away. He was pulling me away from the Beils and I was struggling to get away from him.

1

However, he at last got me away. Sid ran out of the house because, I suspect, of all the shouting and crying. I have never seen Sid again.

We walked, or he pulled me, back to Haywards Heath. It eventually became clear that this man was in fact my elder brother, who was six years older than myself, which made his age to be 14. His name was Percy Sidney Charles Goddard, and he was taking me back to my natural parents. We arrived at a flat in Commercial Square which is in Haywards Heath. My parents were living in one room over a small shop. There was a girl there called Lily who was three years older than myself. I remember still being very upset and crying, and my father took off his belt and I had the first of the many beatings that I was to receive in the years that followed.

I made several attempts to escape and return to my foster parents in Wivelsfield, but each time either my father or brother would catch me before I was able to go very far. Each time I tried to run away ended with another beating, and as time passed I stopped trying. In fact I did not see my foster parents again until much later in life.

My father ruled the family and my brother was his idol. He never carried out any errands, these were left to me. My sister Lily and I got on very well together. I remember once when she tried to prevent my father beating me he turned on her. If I went on an errand for my father I often got belted for not returning straight away – in fact for any silly reason.

Within a few months of returning to Haywards Heath, we moved to 15 Gower Road in the same town. This was a semi-detached three-bedroomed house with a small box room. My parents let the front ground floor room and the front first floor bedroom to a Mr and Mrs Howell who had just married. Soon after we moved there my father brought home a puppy which we named Gip. As we grew up together we had great times together, and I became more settled and happier because of Gip.

My father worked as a labourer mainly on the new London to Brighton A23, and he walked from Haywards Heath to the Bolney area. He was a heavy beer drinker. My mother took in

2

washing and I had an old bicycle on which I could lay the baskets of linen and push them along. I collected the dirty washing before going to school, returning with the clean linen in the evenings.

There were two schools in Haywards Heath, St Wilfrid's Church school and the Council school. I restarted my schooling at the Council school which was situated to the left-hand side of today's shopping precinct in Sussex Road. The school had two iron gates approximately three feet wide. The left-hand gate was the girls' entrance and the right-hand gate was for the boys' entrance. I was caught swinging on the boys' gate by the caretaker named Mr Randell and the next morning, after prayers in the main assembly hall, my name was called out to go up to see the headmaster.

Mr Freestone laid me across a desk and caned me in front of other pupils at the school. I never heard of any other pupils being caned for the same offence while I was there. Talking in class was also punishable with the cane.

There was a small yard at the rear end of Gower Road, and my father decided to keep and train racing pigeons, which was classed at that time as a poor man's sport. This became another job for me.

Taking several pigeons out in a basket, which I tied on the carrier of my bicycle, to various distances from home, I would release the pigeons, making a note of the time and the place, and my father would check in the time they arrived home and entered the pigeon loft. The distance would be increased for the same set of pigeons. The distances would start at Muster Green and finish at Bolney. For the final stage of training I would take the pigeons to the railway station. I would pay the guard to make a note of the time and place where he would release the pigeons. He would put this information on a piece of paper, fold it up and attach it under the ring of one of the pigeon's legs. The pigeon basket would be brought back to Haywards Heath station on his return trip, and I would collect it from there.

When I was about ten or eleven years old, I started a paper round for Brown's newsagents in Sussex Road in Haywards Heath. The round covered Ashenground Road, Wood Ride,

3

Park Road, Haywards Road and Gower Road, for which I received 1s 6d per week. Out of this I had to give my mother one shilling and I kept sixpence.

About this time I became very interested in flying. I would see the occasional plane go over – I must say they were very few and far between in those days. My lady teacher, Miss Lee, was also very interested in flying, and it was arranged between the teacher and my parents for her to take me to the RAF Hendon air display. This was about 1929–30 and was the first time I had seen an aeroplane on the ground or flying so low over the ground. I was determined from that day that one day I would fly – I never realised how near that day would be.

Soon after this event I saw an advertisement in the *Mid-Sussex Times* for Allen Cobbin's Air Circus, which was going to be at a site between Ditchling and Hassocks in Sussex, about six miles from Haywards Heath. Flights were advertised at five shillings a trip. As this event would not take place for about another three months, I decided to save my sixpence a week to take a trip.

About this time a young married couple named Jimmy and Susan Dinnage took over a cycle shop at 44 Sussex Road, Haywards Heath. At the rear of the shop was a wood-built workshop which became a cycle repair shop. The cycle mechanic was a man named Les Sturgon who lived in Kents Road. My paper round took me past this shop every morning, and I remember looking in the window and admiring the new BSA cycles priced at £3 19s 6d. I remember Jimmy and Susan owned a Lancia wire-wheeled car which used to stand on the forecourt. Jimmy had a petrol pump installed on this forecourt and was advertising for a Saturday boy to wind the handle to serve the petrol. I took this job as it fitted in very well with my early paper round. When I was not serving petrol I helped Les in the cycle repair shop. There were not many cars about in those days. What I earned I gave to my mother, and I was now given back one shilling a week. This enabled me to save my five shillings for the forthcoming flight much quicker. Also the knowledge I gained from the cycle repairs was to come in very handy in the future.

4

I became friendly with a Mr Gilbert Kent, who lived almost opposite our house at 4 Gower Road. Mr Kent was a self-employed carpenter with a small workshop behind the house. He also had a larger workshop, built of wood, at the lower end of Gower Road, about where Setyres is situated today, and where he employed two carpenters. Mr Kent always wore riding breeches with brown boots and brown leggings which were kept highly polished. He was the only person up to that time who I saw wearing such clothes. I took every chance I could to watch the men at work. I would do any clearing up and small jobs just out of interest. Mr Kent invited me to go over to his small workshop behind the house and help him in the evenings making coffins when he had an order from the undertakers. When the coffin was made, we used to deliver it to the house after dark in the evening on an iron-wheeled handcart. As the roads were tarred with flint chippings, you can imagine the noise from the iron wheels.

The day arrived for my flight with Allen Cobbin's Circus. It was on a very nice summer's day, and I remember cycling down to the site, which was two flat fields. I suspect they were rented out for the day by a local farmer. There were large queues of people waiting for their turn for a flight. I joined the queue and waited for what seemed years. However, my turn came at last and I remember the man who was taking the money was somewhat surprised that a young lad such as myself would be going up on my own. I almost thought he was not going to let me go – but he did. The liner was a Handley Page with about 20 seats. It was a twin-engine type and constructed mainly in ribbed aluminium. The flight was very enjoyable and lasted about 15 minutes. This first flight confirmed my thoughts that one day I would learn to fly myself.

As I was now coming to the age of 13 and had by now decided I would like to be a carpenter, Mr Kent told me he would gladly take me on as an apprentice when I left school. He asked me if I would like a job as a 'stop-boy' for pheasant-shooting at the Kleinworts' estate. I did not know anything about this 'stop-boy' work. The Kleinworts had a very large estate each side of the Brighton Road which is now called Isaacs Lane. I

5

went to see Mr Hallet, who was the head gamekeeper and lived in the gamekeeper's lodge.

The pheasant shooting was carried out during the winter months, approximately from October to February or March. The winters seemed very much colder than those of today. I was to be there at five on the Saturday morning. I would be given two large sandwiches and a bottle of ginger pop and would be paid five shillings a day. When I reported in, an under-gamekeeper would take me out with other stop-boys and instruct me in what I had to do. I decided to take the job and give up the paper round and my job at Dinnages.

I had to leave home at 4.15 in the morning as I had to walk about four miles by road. It was a bitter cold morning with an icy wind blowing. I had a large overcoat with a scarf under my hat and down over my ears. It was a new experience to be walking out that early in the morning as there were very few street lights in those days. When I arrived at the shed behind the gamekeeper's house, Mr Hallet was inside with a hurricane lamp checking in all the stop-boys. Most of these came from Burgess Hill. There could have been about 50 boys. Some of the boys were only about eight or nine years old, and if any boy was about two minutes late he was sent home. There were always a few more boys who had already signed in on chance. A gamekeeper would take us out to the woods. On each side of the wood he would place a boy to walk up and down and keep tapping with a stick to keep the pheasants in the wood. This would entail four boys to each wood. If I was lucky enough that our wood was one of the early shoots, then we would join in with the beaters. There were about 12 beaters who lined up and beat through the wood with Mr Hallet in front to take control. The pheasants would be driven to the end of the wood, where the shooters would be waiting for them to rise.

There could be about eight to twelve shooters with two double-barrel 12-bore guns with a loader. The guns were lined up and spaced out along the side of the wood. The pheasants had no chance of getting by the guns. I carried out one year as a 'stop-boy' and then beating, for which I received twelve shillings and sixpence a day for the second year. Mr Hallet was given control of the whole operation. Towards the end of the season, he would give the guns orders not to shoot any hen pheasants, the reason for this being that the hens would be spared for breeding in the coming summer. If one of the guns shot a hen bird, Mr Hallet would disqualify him from the shoot that day. Mr Kleinwort was always at the pheasant shoots. He had a very long beard down over the front of his chest. I will mention more about that beard later. When the pheasant-shooting ended I took on two paper rounds for the summer.

I was now coming up to 14 years old and I was looking forward to leaving school and starting work, hopefully as a carpenter apprentice. My life was still not a happy one at home as I became an errand boy for everything that was required at the house. My father still used the belt on me, and Gip was run over and killed, and this upset me for days.

Mr Freestone, the head teacher at the school, called to see my father on several occasions as to why I always appeared very tired and sometimes fell asleep in class. Each time he called my father gave me another hiding. I remember going to Mr Freestone and asking him not to call again to see my parents. He explained to me that he was only trying to help me as the teachers all knew about my home life, and he did not like calling because of the abuse he received from my father.

While I was at this school, I became very interested in cross-country running. I joined the Haywards Heath cross-country running club. We used to train in Victoria Park in the evenings or go out on long runs. This club consisted mainly of men. I ran for the club at Lewes. The cross-country run was 25 miles, but with a shorter route for those under the age of 18. I never came in the first group but was presented with a scarf by the head teacher, Mr Freestone, at the school because it was felt I had made a very good effort for a lad of my age.

My sister was now working as an usherette at the Heath Theatre, which was situated in the Broadway. This theatre, which closed in 1936, is now better known as the old gas showroom site. On Friday evenings I cycled down to this theatre and went to the pictures. I walked home very frightened after seeing a horror film. The next morning I got up to go on my paper round when I realised I had left my bicycle down at the side of the picture house. I walked down to the picture house, only to find the iron gates were closed with a padlock. The gates were about three feet high and on top of the gates were iron hoops. I climbed up on the gate and jumped over. However, I left my right foot in one of the hoops. I hung down on the inside of the gate. I managed to pull myself back up and get off the gate. I then realised I had damaged my right foot, but I still managed to walk home. My parents got a doctor who got me into Haywards Heath cottage hospital. I had a broken ankle! The *Mid-Sussex Times* reporter used to go to the hospital each week for any stories he could find. I made the news that week on the front page and I recovered after a few weeks. I did get my bicycle back because my sister had taken it home for me.

My brother was working for the Central Sussex Electricity company. He was a linesman earning fairly good money. He had always been the idol of my parents and had never carried out any errands or jobs at the house.

As the time for me to leave school was getting near, Mr Kent, who I must mention had had many rows with my father over my home treatment in the past, called to see my parents as regards the apprenticeship. He explained it would be a three-year apprenticeship paying five shillings a week for the first year, ten shillings a week for the second year and fifteen shillings for the third year. It is very hard to explain how I felt when I heard what my parents had to say next. They knew that I was very keen to be a carpenter's apprentice but said that they had already signed indentures with the International Grocery Stores, which was in South Road. This had been done about three months before I was due to leave school, and with no mention about any of this to myself. The first reason they gave for doing this was that if I went to work for Mr Kent there would be tools to purchase throughout the apprenticeship, which they could not possibly afford, whereas with the grocery trade there was very little to provide. Mainly all that was required was a white smock and apron, which would be provided by the firm but washed by my mother. The second reason they gave was that the International would pay ten shillings a week for the first year, fifteen shillings for the second year and one pound for the third year. I was taken round to the stores under protest and forced to sign my name on the indentures.

2

Compulsory Apprenticeship

I left school and started work at the stores. My first week's wages were half a guinea (10s 6d or 52p). Mr Joiner was manager and Mr Shelley was the under-manager. Mr Joiner was a tall man, about six feet. He was always dressed very smartly. Shelley was fairly short and inclined to be slightly bent over; I told him one day he reminded me of the 'Hunchback of Notre Dame'. They were very hard and strict men, and because of my hatred for this kind of work life became more unhappy for me. The other thing which caused me constant trouble throughout the three years was a white shirt with no attached collar but a very hard starched collar which was attached to the shirt with back and front studs. It was agony to get on and even worse to wear. We had to be outside the shop at eight o'clock each morning. Mr Joiner, who lived in the flat over the shop, would open the door. At that time there were about six to eight staff working in the shop.

Very often I had my starched collar in my pocket because I had not had time to fix it on. He would inspect each one for cleanliness, and we would have to hold out our hands in front of him so he could inspect our nails. Any faults found at these inspections would be punished by having to stay evenings after the shop was closed, refilling the shelves in the shop ready for the next day. Mr Joiner and Mr Shelley would spend their evenings in the Sussex Hotel. The shop would be locked up until they returned. This caused problems between my father and Joiner because many evenings I was not home to carry out the jobs I was expected to do.

It was during the first few months of my starting work that my parents decided to move to Victoria Road to a house named 'Woodlands'. There were nearly two acres of land with the house. It was situated at the lower end of the road. There was no built-up road then, and at most times throughout the year one had to walk out to the main road through mud. This caused more problems for me when I was inspected at the stores each morning.

In Franklynn Road was a builder's yard owned by a man called White, who owned a lot of property in and around Haywards Heath. He owned Woodlands, and I understand he offered to sell it to my parents for £800. They would be paying him one pound a week to buy, or if they did not wish to buy, pay one pound a week rent. They would not buy it because of having to look after and pay out to maintain the place.

While working at the International during my early first year there was an electricity pole carrying electric cables which I now know was 400 volts. I remember seeing a linesman electrocuted on the pole which was in Franklynn Road just outside the Sussex Hotel. The man was still at the top of the pole laying back in his safety belt. The power had been switched off. It was later that day before they could get the body down; this was about 1930–31.

My first months at the shop were spent mainly in the warehouse at the back, weighing and packing up all kinds of groceries that were delivered to the warehouse in bulk, such as sugar, cereals and all kinds of dried fruits. These would then be stacked on shelves in the warehouse awaiting the refill of the shelves in the shop. I had to keep my eyes on the shelves in the shop and refill them when required. Also this was to help me to get used to being behind the counter. I still had no interest at all in this work. Shelley was in charge of the grocery counter. I became rebellious to everything he told me to do. Sometimes, in those early days, I would strike out at him. This I only did mainly in the warehouse when there were only the two of us in. Although we were both short, I began to realise that I was much stronger than he was. About every six weeks to two months an

11

inspector would come down from London and spend a day at the shop. During that day he would give me certain tests to do. I cannot remember passing any of the tests.

The situation was that they could sack me only for stealing and I would not resort to doing that, although many a time I was on the verge – only I realised that it would go against my character for the rest of my life. On the other hand, I could not leave, as the apprenticeship had to be completed.

In Victoria Road there were about six pairs of semi-detached cottages, and opposite these were some wooden ex-army buildings all owned by the builders. The cottages and the wooden buildings were in a deplorable condition. There was no maintenance carried out on any of the properties. Between Eastern Road and Western Road was a brickfield which was also owned by the Franklynn Road builders. Below the cottages in Victoria Road was a small bungalow which was rented by the foreman of the brickyard, Mr Phil Jenner. The grounds in Woodlands stretched from what would now be the lower end of Holly Road out to Franklands Wood. There was no Dellney Avenue or Holly Road or Franklands Village. Mainly the area surrounding Victoria Road was forest bushes and bracken. In the grounds at Woodlands were about 40 fruit trees, mainly apples, plum and pear, and also one cherry tree. Before my parents moved to Woodlands, Mr Jenner had lived there and had planted the fruit trees. My parents started to keep pigs, geese, turkeys and had large chicken runs. All this meant more work for me before going to work and evenings when I was not working at the shop; although we were forced to stay some evenings at the shop, this did not entail any extra money.

My mother now took in more washing because of the extra drying ground. This meant more deliveries and collections, some of which I had to take on Sundays. Also, on Sundays I had to go around Haywards Heath collecting pig's food. I had a sack on my cycle, and when this was full I would take it back home and return for more. On Sundays, I could make up to three or four trips, and some Sundays I would be lucky to get my dinner by four o'clock in the afternoon.

One chap, who lived in Station Road, used to collect the food

12

from his neighbours. He had quite a large family. As a repay-ment, I had to supply him each week with a gallon of dead spar-rows which he made into sparrow pies for the family. At home, I would lay some chicken food around on the ground, and down would come the sparrows and I would fire one barrel of the 12-bore shotgun into the sparrows and collect a gallon bucket of sparrows.

Over the past years going back before I left school, any opportunity I had I would go to the Wesleyan Sunday school and church in Perrymount Road. The teachers there were very kind and although I was not able to go very often I was always made welcome. The Pastor at that time was Mr Langridge, who lived in Eastern Road. At the back of Mr Langridge's house was a long brick building which Mrs Langridge used as a laun-dry. This building, after modernisation, is now a printers' shop called Griffin House Printers. Mr Langridge used to wheel the baskets of laundry to the customers the same as I did for my mother.

Mr Langridge was by trade a carpenter who worked for Muzzel and Hiltons in Gower Road. He left them and started up on his own as a builder. Eventually, he built most of the houses in Dellney Avenue and Holly Road. When these roads were built we were able to go out from Woodlands to Franklynn Road. This was much better than Victoria Road, as there was no hard road yet. Victoria Road was then known as one of the worst roads in Haywards Heath. Some of the families who lived in the cottages and wooden huts were very hard and lived very rough. It was classed as a very unsafe road to venture through after dark. It was somewhat of a relief to be able to avoid that way out. However, in the next few years I was to get to know some of the families much better.

It was in the early 1930s that I became interested in wireless. To be able to receive any reception at all it was necessary to have a pole erected in the garden with an aerial wire from the top of the pole to a high point on the house, down into the sitting room and connected into the wireless set. I carried out several of these installations for friends. I enjoyed doing any work such as this. As there was no electricity in the road at that time, sets were operated with a dry high-tension battery – 120 volts DC and a wet accumulator of about 2.5 volts which was re-chargeable on a weekly basis. If the accumulator went flat before the next one was delivered, then we had no wireless.

My father hated music, so the wireless was not allowed to be on when he was in the house. This seemed very strange to me as my mother was a trained pianist and singer, although we had no piano at that time.

The living conditions at Woodlands were very primitive compared with those of today. There was a cold-water tap over a sink in the kitchen. In the corner was a copper bowl which held about ten or twelve gallons of water. This was installed when the house was built, with a fire grate under the bowl and a chimney built out through the roof. It was used about three times a week for boiling the washing and on Saturdays for bathing. It was another job for me to light the fire and fill the copper. This I had to do before leaving for work in the morning. The gas was used for lighting and cooking. There were gas points in the kitchen, sitting room and front rooms, which were lit by a mantel. As there was no lighting in the bedrooms, we took our own candles each night. Although there were fire-places in all the rooms, the only one that was ever used was in the sitting room.

During the winters, the bedrooms were very cold, when there were severe frosts the windows would be covered in fern ice. This could remain for days and even weeks. However hard the conditions were, we kept quite healthy. There was a long shaped tin bath which hung on the outside wall, this I brought into the kitchen for bathing. On Saturdays, I would have filled the copper with water and lit the fire. I would get the tin bath, put more cold water in the copper, which would be used by each one to warm up the existing water in the bath. My mother and father would bath first, my brother next, my sister and then myself. When I had finished, I would empty the bath with the jug and hang it back on the wall outside.

At 15 years old, I had completed my first year of the apprenticeship. I still had no interest. In fact an inspector came down from London to give me my first yearly test, which I

14

failed completely, and I was still in trouble with my starched collar.

The next year was spent on the grocery counter serving customers and having fights with Shelley. It was about this time that Joiner, the manager, retired. He moved out of the flat and away from Haywards Heath. Soon after this, Shelley got a transfer to another shop in Kent. The new manager was a Mr Cadman, who treated the staff as human beings. In fact life became more pleasant at the shop. The new under-manager, Mr Reynolds, was also a very kind man. Both of these worked on the provisions counter. I was looking forward to my third year as I would then be on this counter.

Mr Cadman, who was married, moved into the flat. His wife was a specialist in making home-made long jam Swiss rolls. Mr and Mrs Cadman came down to Woodlands to see the apple trees and asked if they could come down to the grounds for a picnic. They often had a picnic, and Mrs Cadman always made Swiss rolls for my mother.

Opposite the shop in South Road was another grocery stores called Home and Colonial Stores. At that time there was a price war going on between the Co-op stores in Sussex Road, Home and Colonial and the International. If Mr Cadman wanted to know the price of certain things in the window opposite, I had to walk down the other side of the road and make a note of certain prices I saw in the window. I may have to walk past several times to gather all the information he required.

One morning, as I was outside the shop opposite, two of the staff from the Home and Colonial came out, grabbed me and pulled me into their shop. I was warned by their manager that if I was caught doing this again I would get a damned good hiding. As it was, I got a clip round the earhole when they let me go, and that was the last time I went price-tagging.

Inspectors from London used to visit the shop about every three months. There was no warning as to when. One day an inspector walked into the shop as Mr Reynolds was cutting some cooked ham on the bacon machine, and a small piece fell off the machine onto the counter. At that moment he picked it up and ate it, and the inspector saw him do this and he was given one minute's notice. Mr Reynolds had been with the International Stores for 18 years and he was waiting to be promoted to a manager's job at another branch. I mention this to try to illustrate how strict discipline was in those days.

One of my jobs at the shop was on Saturday afternoon: I had to go out with a trade bicycle with a basket filled with offcuts of bacon and any other ends of cooked meats that would not keep until the Monday. These I would sell for about threepence each – or more if I could. Most of these I would sell to the people who lived in the cottages and huts in Victoria Road. It was because of this that I came to know these people better. In fact I became friendly with most of these families, and realised they were not as bad as people outside the road thought them to be.

Many of the apples from the orchard at Woodlands were purchased by Mr Cadman for resale in the shop. Livestock was purchased by the public. The fowl were got ready for cooking by my mother. Pigs were purchased and resold by Bannisters, the auctioneers, at the Haywards Heath market, which was on the site where Sainsburys is today.

At 16, I again failed my yearly test at the stores. I moved on to the provision counter, which was more interesting. This was now the last year of my apprenticeship. I now received one pound a week, of which I kept five shillings, and with this extra money I had to buy my own clothes. On the provisions counter I learnt to pat butter and margarine which was carried out at the customer's request. Also, I had to bone and cut up sides of bacon. Although I have never done anything like this since, I feel that I could still carry out these operations now. I wonder how many so-called grocers could carry out these tasks today.

Because I was now much happier, the third year of my apprenticeship seemed to pass more quickly. I still disliked the work, and eventually my last day arrived. This day was spent with an inspector who was giving me my final test and observing me serving customers on both counters. The last test was after the shop closed. He gave me a list of groceries which I had to put together, make up the account and parcel these items into a brown paper parcel and tie it up. I was used to a normal

16

amount of groceries, but this was a maximum amount to get it tied up after a fashion. He picked up the parcel to move it onto another counter, and the whole lot fell to pieces onto the floor. He was in a raving temper. I just stood and laughed, took off my smock and apron and threw them onto the floor, gave him one week's notice and walked out of the shop. I had known for a long time what I would do the day my apprenticeship finished. The next week was not a happy one at home because of what I had done, and at that time I did not have another job to go to when I finished at the shop the following Saturday.

3

Gathering War Clouds

During that week when I was working out my notice, I managed to creep out the back way of the shop and go to the Central Sussex Electricity Company which was situated in the Broadway. I had found out that if I was interested in football, I would stand a very good chance of getting a job.

I was lucky enough to see a Mr Smith and a Mr Crowther, who were engineers at that time. It was Mr Smith who managed the CSEC football team. I had never played football, as my sport then was cross-country running. They told me they were looking for a lad such as myself to go out with a surveyor mapping out the land for the erection of high-tension lines. Mr Smith asked me if I played football. I replied that I had not played football but had been a linesman at several matches. They took me on to start the following Monday, and the following Saturday I was linesman at their ground at Oathall Avenue. I really did not know what I was doing, but Mr Smith was quite happy.

Mr Smith was a short man who, unfortunately, had an impediment – talking through his nose. Crowther was very tall and belonged to some strange religion which did not allow him to swear, drink or read newspapers. When he was upset, Crowther would walk up and down a small passage outside the office with his hands behind his back. I was in the passage once when the office door opened and Smith said to Crowther, 'Why the hell don't you have a bloody good swear-up and clear it off your chest? Then come back in

18

the office and get some work done!' All this, of course, coming through his nose!

The surveyor, Mr Spy, picked me up on the Monday morning. He was surveying for high-tension lines around the south of Sussex. My job was to pull the measuring chain and to hold the rods up. He would use a theodolite. Although the job was not at all interesting, Mr Spy loved mushrooms and some days we would spend picking. When he had enough, he would sort them out, keeping all the best for himself and I could have the rest. He wore plus fours or knickerbockers, as they were called then. He had holes in the trouser pockets, and when we surveyed through a chicken farm he always came out with eggs around the legs of the plus fours. He had an old Delage car. It was a two-door with two seats in the front and a dickey seat in the back. This had a lift-up door which provided two seats in the open. Many a time I had to sit in the dickey when it was raining and sometimes snowing.

One morning, we stopped at the general post office in Boltro Road. Mr Spy came out and started the car, which then caught fire. There was a Carter Paterson delivery van standing behind us. The driver put out the fire, which was mainly around the engine, with his own fire extinguisher. There was an argument afterwards as to why Mr Spy would not pay the cost of the extinguisher. I was very happy to help him to get the car back on the road again.

One dark evening in the middle of winter, we finished work at Ashington, a small village nearby, and left to go home. It was snowing hard, and soon after we left the car stopped and would not start again. Neither Spy nor myself had any money to call a garage, so we stopped a passing car and asked if they would ask the next garage to send someone to us. A breakdown lorry arrived some hours later and towed us into Bucks Barn Garage. They told Spy he would have to leave the car there for repair, and at the same time they insisted he pay for the towing. In the end he sold them the car for £5. After paying for the towing, he had just enough for our bus fares home. That was the last we saw of the Delage.

About this time, a Mr Beecham, a projectionist at the Heath

19

Theatre, through my sister asked if I could help him some evenings in the projection room. This entailed rewinding the spools of films once they had been shown. The Broadway cinema was opened in 1932 and later re-named Union Cinema in 1937. The projection room was at the rear of the screen, unlike the normal projection room at the front. There were several reasons for this, the main one was that the film was not being shown through smoke. After the newsreel had been shown at the Heath, I had to take it to the Broadway for it to be shown there. Many times, because I rewound the reel the wrong way, it would start showing upside down. I never seemed to get it right. We had many breakdowns on the old projectors. At the Heath, Mr Beecham would join two reels together to save another change-over from one machine to the other. This meant the spool was very overloaded. One evening, we had so many breakdowns we were in fear of being lynched by the audience. We had just changed over to the machine that had an overloaded spool when the film came off the take-up spool at the bottom of the machine. Rather than stop the film, I took the end out of the projection box and out onto the pavement in the Broadway. I stood outside pulling the film through two doors and piling it into a heap about four feet high.

Mr Beecham wanted me to become his assistant as the Heath Theatre was closing on 30 May 1936 and the Perrymount was being opened the same day. I helped out in the projection box at the Perrymount for one week when it opened. As there was so much temporary wiring, there were two firemen in the box with us. I did not fancy working every evening, and my full job was still with CSEC.

When I was not required by Mr Spy, who had to spend days and sometimes weeks in the office once we had completed a survey, Mr Smith arranged for me to go out with one of the servicing gangs. This work entailed installing the supply wires from the road poles into the houses. For this work one had to use iron climbers to go up wooden poles. Soon I became quite an expert at going up and down poles, and then lost my job with Mr Spy.

The next two years, until I became 19, I spent with the CSEC

20

working in the low-tension lines which carried 400 volts. I was now classed as an assistant electrical linesman so, coupled with my running the line at football matches, I was a linesman whatever way I looked at it.

Although life was still not a happy one at home with my father, I was beginning to stand on my own two feet and refusing to carry out all they expected me to do. I was still very interested in wireless, in fact I purchased my own accumulator charger with which I could charge up about six accumulators at one time. This I did for friends in the cottages and charged them sixpence a time.

About this time a firm of electrical contractors came into Haywards Heath from Scotland. They had contracts to build the high-tension lines which I had helped Mr Spy to survey a few years before. These lines were carrying 11,000 volts and would be constructed between towns and villages in Sussex.

My brother left the CSEC and worked for the contractors. He was working at Newhaven when he purchased a new BSA Blue Star 350cc motorcycle. One evening, coming home, the road had been re-tarred and covered with flint chippings, and the motorcycle slipped on the flints. My brother was not hurt but never rode a motorcycle again. I purchased the motorcycle from my brother. This became my pride and joy. My sister was now married and moved out of home and took a housekeeper's job in Bath. I very often used to visit them. This was a long trip to take in those days. The motorcycle gave me a lot of enjoyment. I felt free to come and go as I pleased. This caused more arguments with my parents to the extent that I decided to leave home.

I gave up my job on the CSEC and went to work for a family who owned Glebe House in Denmans Lane, Lindfield, as an odd-job boy. The reason I took this job was because I could live in. The lady at Glebe House employed a chauffeur and a maid. The maid lived in and was only allowed one half day a week free time on a Wednesday afternoon, but she had to be at the house to make tea and then the rest of the evening was again her own time. I have mentioned this to give some idea of the times we were living in.

The chauffeur lived in Sunte Avenue and I was helping him one evening to move some bags of cement from Glebe House to his own house. We drew up in the drive of Glebe House by the stables. He switched off the engine, and in the headlights of the car we saw something moving on the gravel drive. It took a little while to distinguish what it was. Two rats were carrying an egg. One was lying on his back, holding the egg in his four legs and the other rat was pulling him along by his tail. Later in life, I saw an illustration in a book of the same thing and thought how lucky I was to have seen this being performed. The job at Glebe House only lasted three weeks. My father came to see me and told me it was making my mother ill because I had moved out. I agreed to go back on condition that I would not carry out any more work at Woodlands.

My mother then gave up taking in washing and the number of pigs was reduced, so I no longer collected in their food. With no trouble at all I started work at the contractors as an assistant linesman.

There were two gangs carrying out the building of the high-tension lines in Sussex. The foreman of the gang I was with was named Mr Carter. He had a motorcycle with a sidecar and had lodgings in Ashenground Road. Where a new line was started, the first job was to dig the holes for the poles to be erected in, these were six feet deep. Each hole was expected to be dug out by lunchtime. If the digging was fairly easy, then we would have to dig two holes each day. The pole holes had to be excavated so that the pole would be erected exactly where the peg was in the ground. All poles had to be in a straight line from angle poles across the countryside. In one pole hole I had started to dig the farmer had buried a cow about two months before. I had to dig my hole through the dead cow. Mr Carter agreed to pay me extra money, but with one condition. Now, Mr Carter smoked a pipe, and any favour shown to anyone had to be compensated by supplying him with one or two ounces of St Bruno tobacco. Out of the extra money I had to buy two ounces. I do not remember him ever buying his own. After the pole was erected and made safe, I had to fill the hole back in myself.

We were working near the village of Henfield. We had a coke brazier on the roadside, and everyone was sitting around having tea and our midday break. A girl came down the road and stood talking. She was Scottish and was down here on holiday with an aunt. As Mr Carter was also Scottish, they were having a long conversation, during which it turned out she had not been anywhere, just staying in Henfield with the aunt.

Mr Carter instructed me to turn up the next day with my motorcycle and take the girl out on the pillion to see some of the country. This I did and took her along the south coast road out to Dover, stopping at various places along the way. I returned inland and it made a very nice day out on full pay. The next day Mr Carter wanted to know all the details of the day out, which I told him, and also informed him I was putting in for two hours overtime on my timesheet. This he agreed to, but with the usual request for two ounces of St Bruno.

My mother had by now purchased a piano and a piano accordion. Most Saturday evenings were spent in one of the pubs. The favourite was the Liverpool Hotel, which was situated at the lower end of Station Road opposite the entrance to the lower line of Haywards Heath railway station. On the other side of the station was the Haywards Hotel. My mother would play either the piano or the accordion. The other pub she sometimes played at was the Star. There were not many pubs that allowed singing. This was really the only entertainment in those days. I did play darts at the Sussex Hotel, but was really not very good. I loved shove-halfpenny – in fact I palled up with a chap named Johnny Turk and we played this game as a double, and there were not many could beat us. Beer was fourpence a pint. We used to play for half-pints and many evenings, because of our winnings at shove-halfpenny, it did not cost us anything.

I also smoked, and Woodbine cigarettes were fourpence for ten or five in a packet for twopence. Sometimes I would have five Woodbines. We played in most pubs in Haywards Heath, Cuckfield and Lindfield. I very often went to the cinemas and also to the Hippodrome in Brighton. I never missed many Max Miller or the Crazy Gang shows. Other shows I remember

23

seeing were Arthur Tracey, the street singer and Michael Holliday. This was the extent of my night life.

I used to catch the last train home from Brighton, which arrived in Haywards Heath about eleven-thirty. At night I walked from the station to my home and was always stopped by a foot patrol policeman as to where I had been and where I was going.

Work with the Scottish contractors was now becoming short, as one line was completed it might be a break of several days before the next line was due to begin. We were told at one stage that it would be about three weeks before another line was due to begin. I tried to get back on the CSEC, but was told there would not be a vacancy for about three weeks, so I decided to sign on the dole. I joined the queue outside the dole office in Commercial Square, and a chap named Ernie Welfare, who I know very well, came out of the office and we had a chat. Ernie had been given a blue card to go to the horse riding school which was behind the Star Hotel. They required a man to carry out general work with the horses. He did not want the job and asked me if I was interested. I told him I only wanted a job temporary, so it was arranged I would go up and see if I could get the job before Ernie got there.

Ernie had to go, as his name was on the blue card. However, I walked to the stables, which were just under a mile from the dole office. I told the man who was in charge that I had heard he wanted a yard man. He explained that the Labour Exchange was sending a man up. I told him how disappointed I was and had always looked forward to the day when I could work with horses. I believe he felt sorry for me and he gave me the job. When Ernie walked in about the job, I was sweeping the yard up. Later, Ernie thanked me and bought me a drink. In fact I enjoyed the work, which was quite hard and I learnt to ride early mornings when exercising. I stayed for about four weeks and then went back to the CSEC.

Now that I had reached the age of 20 in 1936, I started courting a girl who lived in West Street, Burgess Hill, by the name of Dorothy Leaney. I got on very well with her father, who was a very good darts player. I would go down to see 'Dot' as we called her, but would call in the Cricketers pub at the top of West Street. If her father was in I sometimes stayed with him, playing darts the whole evening. This caused trouble between Dot and myself, and we would not see each other for long spells but always seemed to get back together again. This went on for several years. Looking back now, I believe my only love at that stage of my life was for anything electrical, wireless or mechanical.

My brother got married about this time in my life. I was best man. At the reception I met a relation of my new sister-in-law, who was a very bad cripple. We had a long conversation, during which I learnt that he lived in Lewes and was a self-employed shoe repairer. He invited me down to Lewes and I would watch him at work. He asked me if I would like to learn the trade. I replied I would very much like to learn but would not be interested to carry it out for a living. I went down some evenings and weekends whenever I had the opportunity, until eventually I could repair shoes as well as he. It was all done by hand (no machines). I invested in the tools and repaid him by still going down and helping him out when he wanted me. This again was very useful to me later in life.

One thing I was never interested in was dancing. It had no appeal for me at all.

News had been coming in for some time via the wireless and at the cinemas of Hitler's rise to power in Germany and how the Nazis were treating the Jews in Germany. Everyone was talking about how long it would be for England and Germany to be at war again. It was about this time also that we were hearing about Mussolini the Italian dictator, with his following of Fascist Blackshirts.

During the next year another name was getting into the news – Mosley. He was going round the country, giving talks in local halls, trying to rally up a following of Blackshirts in this country. Through the news we received it was clear he was not being very well received. I never heard of or knew of anyone locally who was a Blackshirt or a follower of Mosley. In fact, there was more of a general hatred, owing to the news from Germany. If there were any followers they kept a low profile, not showing

25

themselves during the following skirmishes. Mosley was booked to come to Burgess Hill to give a speech. Word got around in our pubs in Haywards Heath, asking for support on the evening to oppose this. Many chaps of my age went down to the hall. Mosley had a good support of Blackshirts at the hall that evening. Nevertheless, after a considerable amount of uproar and fighting, Mosley never got onto the stage to speak. It was soon after this that Mosley booked the Public Hall in South Road, Haywards Heath for a meeting. It was arranged with all our supporters to gather outside the hall early and to ensure Mosley would not be able to get out of his car. Three cars pulled up with a considerable number of Mosley Blackshirts. Mosley was in the front car. Some of the Blackshirts got out, and immediately fighting started to get them back in the cars. The cars were being badly damaged. When they realised they were hopelessly outnumbered, they gave up and drove off.

While working back with the CSEC, I went out with an electrician evenings and weekends carrying out house wiring. As electricity was becoming more available in homes there was quite a demand for house wiring. I was very pleased to learn, and it was not long before I was carrying out installations myself. This knowledge was to prove very useful later in life. I was beginning to think that one day I would work for myself.

A friend of mine who, in fact, was an old school pal at the council school, named Ben Westgate, had completed an apprenticeship as a mechanical engineer at Caffyns in the Broadway. Ben was a wizard with anything to do with cars, motorcycles or clocks. He seemed to be able to rectify any faults, even when we were at school the teachers used to bring clocks for Ben to repair. Ben never smoked or drank. The only thing we had in common was our love for engines. Ben married a girl who also was a very good mechanic, and soon after he was married he was transferred to East Grinstead to another Caffyns branch and made a foreman. He rented a house but had very little furniture. There was a bed upstairs and a table and chairs downstairs, no carpets or lino, and a gas cooker in the kitchen. I spent some weekends with Ben and his wife; there were engines in

26

almost every room. We would work on the engines all the time. We would buy eggs, bread and butter when we were hungry. We lived on fried eggs!

We would leave early on Sunday mornings to go to Pride and Clark's in London for any spares we required. I was now enjoying life for the first time, but the clouds were closing in.

There was talk that conscription would soon be introduced into the armed forces. Instructions were being given out how to build an air raid shelter in your own back garden. It was expected that war would break out any day. It was in September 1938 that Neville Chamberlain came back from Germany, waving a piece of paper and announcing that he had secured 'peace in our time' after signing the Munich pact. Very few people believed this. Hitler was still taking over countries around Germany, the Jews were being treated very badly, according to the news we were receiving, and there was the Hitler Youth. These were babies born from typical blond, blue-eyed Teutonic parents.

I felt the time had come for me to sell my motorcycle. I had very bad teeth and was having three or four out by cocaine by a dentist in South Road, named Mr Edgar German. He had started his practice in about 1925 and caused quite a stir locally. When he first started, he was travelling down from London and always wore a top hat and morning coat. He had just completed taking out 17 of my teeth, and I would have to wait six months for the gums to settle down before impressions could be taken for making top and bottom dentures. On completion he would bill me for the whole job – this would be in about February 1939.

It was near the end of October 1938, on a Saturday morning, I received a letter to go to the council school to collect a gas mask. My family were to go later that morning. I well remember when I arrived at the school, looking at the iron gate that I had been caught swinging on several years before, and realising this was decision time. I decided to go down to the army recruiting office. This was situated on the site where Sainsburys is today. On the way down I called in the CSEC offices. Mr Smith was in, and I informed him of my intentions. I really did not believe I would be accepted because of the state of my teeth and my poor education. It would have been a disappointment if I had been rejected, as the war clouds were expected to burst any day. This also was a very good reason for leaving home.

On arriving at the office, which was a room in the hall where the Territorials carried out training, I was rather surprised to be the only one. However, I knew the recruiting officer, as he used the Heath Hotel and I had very often had a chat with him over a drink. After writing down particulars about myself, he asked me if I had any choice, which branch of the services I would like to go in. My answer was the Air Force. He replied that was out of the question, owing to my poor education and having no certificates. He did explain to me that if I went into any branch of the services there would be ample opportunity for me to further my education and to obtain certificates, which might help me to gain a transfer into another branch.

I was not keen to go into the infantry, but would be happy at second best to be in any branch which was mechanical. He then looked at me and remarked that a small chap like me – as I was only five feet four inches tall – would fit into a tank very well. He assured me that, once I was enlisted, I would receive the best of dental treatment. He suggested I should go home and let my parents know what I was doing and come back to him. This I refused, as now I had made up my mind I did not wish anyone to talk me out of it. As he would no doubt see my father in the Heath that evening, he would let him know. I was not really worried about that anyway. He issued me a railway warrant to Brighton and instructions to report in at Preston Park Barracks.

4

Enlisting and Training

At Preston Park I came under the supervision of a Colour Sergeant who informed me I would be staying there over that weekend and there would be certain tests I would need to carry out on the Sunday. Providing I passed out OK, I would be on my way on the Monday. At that particular moment I had no idea where. I was told I would have to work for my keep that weekend, such as chopping wood, getting coal in, clearing out the fireplaces and lighting fires in the morning, cleaning up two rooms and cleaning boots.

On the Sunday I was given certain other tests to carry out. The main one I remember was to sit at a table with something under a cloth in front of me. I was told that when given the word I was to remove the cloth and re-assemble what was under it, I would be timed as to how long it would take me. When I removed the cloth there was a spring-type washing peg – two wood side pieces with the centre spring. I was not very long putting the peg together. I was informed later that many who had taken the same test had not been able to assemble the peg.

I passed all my tests OK and was told I would be sworn in on the Monday morning and put on a train to Bovington, where I would start my training in the Royal Tank Corps. I had no idea where Bovington was until told it was in Dorset. On the Monday morning, 1 November 1938, I rose early to carry out the various jobs I had to do. I had a very good breakfast as I was told I would be travelling most of that day, then taken to an office where I signed papers to serve six years with the colours

29

and six years on reserve. I was then sworn in and given the King's Shilling. Soon after this the Colour Sergeant, now dressed up in his full regimental uniform and carrying a flying Union Jack flag, marched me from the barracks to Brighton station. As I was on my own, I felt a right ninny. He got me my ticket, came onto the platform and wished me luck as he opened the carriage door to make sure I was on that train. He waited on the platform until the steam train pulled out. I was on my own in that carriage for the whole journey. During this time I began to wonder if I had really done the right thing, as 12 years was a terrible long time, but now there was no turning back. This was going to be the longest train journey I had travelled. It was a horrible November day, and I cannot remember the time we left Brighton but feel it was about eleven a.m. The station I was to arrive at was called Wool in Dorset.

At about three in the afternoon I started to worry that I had missed the station. When we stopped at the next station I asked a porter and he replied that I should arrive at Wool at about four-thirty, which we did.

When I got out it was quite dark with a strong wind blowing and driving rain, which I came to know later as typical moors weather. I was surprised how small Wool station was. I had been told back in Brighton that there would be someone to meet me there. It was not long before a chap in uniform asked if my name was Goddard. He told me he had been instructed to come down to pick me up and take me to the camp. He also said, 'I'll tell you, old friend, you can take my advice and get over to the other platform and catch the next train back.' It was poor advice, as I realised that, having been sworn in, I would then have become a deserter before I had really started.

By the time we arrived at the camp, which was only two or three miles from the station, my heart was in my boots as I was doomed for disaster, according to him. He left me at the guard room, from where I was escorted to a wooden army hut. This hut had very nice carpets, armchairs, nice beds and pictures of tanks on the walls. We thought how comfortable it was. There were a number of chaps who had recently arrived. We would stay in this reception hut until kitted out with uniforms etc. and then formed up into a squad. This also gave us time to find our way around the camp and watch other squads drilling on the parade grounds.

We were also being given lectures on what to expect once we started our training, and of course the do's and don'ts. We had now received our khaki uniforms, and our squad of about 25 were ready to start training. We were now moved to another hut with no carpets, armchairs or pictures, only beds, which were no way as comfortable as the ones we had left. When we had settled in a Sergeant came in and introduced himself as our squad sergeant. His name was Sergeant Voller. We had to form up outside the hut on the parade ground, where he sorted us out as to our height etc. He was very strict. Every time we were to form up outside the hut we would take the same position as he had arranged us. He thought he was going to have a hard job on his hands to make soldiers out of such a shower of human beings the likes of which he had never seen before!

He ordered us to be outside the hut at five a.m. the next morning, washed, shaved, boots cleaned and with our dixies and utensils ready to march over to the dining room for breakfast. The rest of the day would be spent going to the hairdresser and dentist and an interview with the Commanding Officer, who laid out what would be expected from me over the next nine months. This would be the length of time for my training. I would not be allowed any leave until I had passed all the required tests in three months' time. He advised me to see the paymaster and to make an allowance from my pay each week to be paid to my parents. They could save all or part, so that when I went on leave there would be something there for me. This I did.

For the next two months we were drilled every working day. During the first two weeks I visited the dentist and had impressions taken and plates fitted. I had to persevere wearing them, but they were OK. The weather that winter of 1938–39 was very hard. There was no excuse for not shaving, even when the water pipes were frozen. We had to break the ice on the water tubs outside to shave and wash. During the weeks of squad drilling, at the weekends some of the other chaps who I had

31

become friendly with went for walks over the moors. We had heard the gunnery ranges, where eventually we would be taking a course. They were at Lulworth Cove on the coast, approximately five miles south of Bovington camp and 20 miles east of Weymouth. One Sunday, we decided to walk to the cove. This was to become one of our favourite spots to spend Sundays when we had no money. There was nothing at all at the cove in those days, unlike today, as it is now very commercialised.

At the back of the camp were the tank training grounds, which have not changed very much over the years, except there is now a hard road built alongside the mud tracks. Along the public road, which runs along the side of the tank training ground, is a spot called Clouds Hill, where still stands the cottage where Lawrence of Arabia lived. He did enlist for a short time in the Tank Corps as it was then called, but could not put up with the strict discipline. After two years he transferred to the RAF. His army number in the tank corps was 7875698 when he enlisted in 1923, 15 years later mine was 7889792. About one mile from the cottage is the spot where he was killed on his motorcycle.

In our squad there was a Canadian chap who was very disliked by everyone in the hut. Someone was always losing something from their locker. We were sure he was a born thief. Sergeant Voller was always having trouble with him, and he had been up in front of the Commanding Officer for different offences. He always seemed to be picking on me, perhaps because I was one of the smallest chaps in the squad. One evening, things came to a head between him and myself and a fight started. The other chaps were shouting and backing me up. There was quite a lot of blood, I believe from bleeding noses. A sergeant passing the hut heard the noise, came in and stopped the fight. Our squad was due for physical training the next day. The sergeant ordered us that before the class started the next day we would be given boxing gloves, and there would be no rounds and it would end when one or the other had given in or was knocked out. I had never worn boxing gloves in my life, but was not too worried, as after the night before I felt fairly confident. I don't know if

32

I knocked him out or if he was shamming, but after I gave him two punches he sat on the floor with his eyes closed until counted out. Very soon after this, he was called up again before the Commanding Officer. We never saw him again. No one ever knew what happened to him.

By the entrance to the camp was a small shop owned by Mr and Mrs Smith. They sold quite a selection of things. There was in the window a toasting fork with a Tank Corps badge on the top. This took my eye, so I went in and enquired as to how much it would cost. It was one shilling and sixpence. All I had in my pocket was sixpence, and that was for me to go to the pictures that evening. I asked if they would reserve it for me until I had all the money. This they could not do, but if I paid them sixpence a week then it would be mine. I never went to the pictures that evening, as I had to leave my sixpence deposit. When I collected the toasting fork after the next two weeks, I saw in the shop a pair of china tanks that also had the Tank Corps crest on each side. I cannot remember the exact price they were, but I believe five shillings the pair. We agreed on one shilling deposit and one shilling a week for the next month. By purchasing these items it meant I had to give up some cigarettes and beer, but it was more than worth it, as you will realise when you read on.

Apart from the drilling on the parade ground, which could take about four hours a day, we had to attend other classes such as physical training, and as I was going to be trained as a tank driver and wireless operator I started to learn Morse. The sergeant who was taking the education classes in the day also gave two evening classes on Tuesday and Wednesday evenings in his hut. I attended these. Eventually, I went up to Salisbury on two occasions to gain my third- and second-class certificates. The next stage was the first-class certificate, which could be gained by passing one subject at a time. As my best subject was arithmetic, I decided to go for that first. It was very hard work, but towards the end of my time at Bovington I went to Salisbury again and passed. The next subject was English, but my study for this came to a sudden end. So much for my dreams of passing the first class and put in for a transfer to the RAF. However,

I was now enjoying the army life although the discipline was strict, but something happened one afternoon later on that eased the discipline a little.

We had now passed out for our drilling, and our squad started on a mechanical course which began with us being taught how a four-cylinder petrol engine worked and going on to understanding everything about an army lorry. This was to be important to us on the last day of our three months' training, when we could go on our first leave. While being taught to drive the lorry, the instructor would make a note of every time I stalled the engine. A penny was then stopped out of my money on payday. When, eventually, I was taught to drive a tank, this was increased to twopence.

It was about two months into my training when I was walking across the parade ground one dark evening, when another recruit passed me. I stopped and called after him, 'Is your name Mick?' and with this he came back and then recognised me and we shook hands. It was in fact Mick Pateman, who lived at North Chailey, a small village about five miles from Haywards Heath. Mick worked for the Lewes Water Board as a plumber, and we had met previously in a pub in Haywards Heath. It was great meeting Mick and we visited each other in our huts, met in the NAAFI and went for a drink together when we had the money.

There were very odd times when we would be given two hours off on an afternoon. We were allowed to rest on our beds. One day the weather was terrible, very cold and snowing, and everyone had to stay in the hut. Then in came Sergeant Voller and ordered everyone to change into shorts and vests as we were going cross-country running round the tank training grounds. We had to assemble at a given point within the next 15 minutes, start off and follow the signs that had already been placed around the course. I had still gone running any chance I had, and was now fitter than ever. The distance was about eight miles, and I had no problem in finishing first. Because of this I was then put into the Bovington cross-country team. It meant life became a little easier. If you were into any sport and would compete against other units you received extra food and time off for training, as well as travelling to various other camps.

I passed my driving test on lorries and started learning to drive tanks. I also started the wireless course. We were now beginning to look forward to the final day of our training, when we would be allowed to wear the Tank Corps blue uniform, which we had to purchase ourselves and which was more comfortable than khaki and smarter. The Royal Tank Corps at that time was the only unit wearing black berets.

Between classes one day we were marched out of the camp and down past Smith's shop and into a small room about 15 feet square. In the centre was a miniature mock-up of the battle of Cambrai. This was the first successful tank battle to take place during the First World War, on 20 November 1917, and is still celebrated very much each year. There were many other small pieces to do with the short history of tanks. This small room was the early days of a museum which is now the largest tank museum in the world – it is well worth a visit.

I palled up with a Scottish chap named McNeil. Mac, as I shall call him, was a quiet chap and softly spoken. I gathered from our conversations that Mac had not enjoyed a happy upbringing, like myself. I believe this was a reason we palled up together. He also enjoyed a drink, and perhaps sometimes we had too much but always got back to camp together. He was very much liked everywhere we went. To go home to Scotland was too far to travel for his first leave, so I invited him to come home with me. Later any weekend leaves he came with me and became well-known in Haywards Heath. I became fairly efficient in Morse, and because of my love for wireless passed out with fairly good marks. In fact, the instructor asked me if I would consider taking a Lance Corporal's stripe. This I turned down, as I was quite happy with the lads. There were times I thought that now the crisis had settled down I had been silly in committing myself for the 12 years. On the other hand, I was fairly happy enjoying the life and at the same time gaining valuable knowledge in many subjects.

About this time some units of cavalry were being mechanised – changing over from horses to tanks. All tank crews had to form up in front of their tanks, and on the order to mount climb to the top and lower ourselves down through the cupola into the tank. The driver would be the first, gunner second, wireless operator who, when the tank was in action would also be loader, was third, and last would be the tank commander. I felt sorry for some of the cavalry chaps who came to Bovington to train on tanks. It was quite a long time before they changed over uniforms and so did not have the black dungarees which were worn when operating in tanks. They had to put up with a lot of remarks from us when mounting the tanks still wearing spurs.

As we were now coming towards the end of our training, we had to decide which battalion we wished to be posted to. There were at that time eight battalions, some in England and some abroad. McNeil and I decided we might as well try and get a holiday abroad and put in for Egypt. When the posting of our squad went up on the posting board we had been posted to the Eighth, stationed in Egypt, for three years. This was something for us to look forward to. Mick Pateman was eventually posted to the Third Battalion, who were stationed at Warminster Camp, Wiltshire.

Although the crisis had settled down temporarily, a lot of preparation was going on. Small batches of the reservists, who had completed their six years with the colours but were now serving six on reserve, were being called back to Bovington.

At long last the day arrived for our final test. We were told that it had to be fully completed before we could collect our free travel warrant tickets and pay. I had purchased a set of secondhand blues from Smith's shop, and these were laid on my bed ready to change into. We were ordered to parade outside the hut at eight and then marched down to the lorry depot. At the depot we were then split into groups of four. Each group was taken out I believe about one mile from the depot to a lorry. We could not see any other lorries or signs of the rest of the squad. The lorry had been set up with faults. I truly cannot remember how many faults – maybe 50 or 60. The examiner who had taken us out to the lorry instructed us to find any faults, rectify them and drive the lorry back to the depot for him to examine. If any faults were still found, we had to drive it back to the spot we had come from and trace the other faults. We were not informed as to how many faults remained. It got into the afternoon, I believe we had driven back to the depot about ten times, but still had faults remaining. The lorry was running perfectly and we were really getting worried, as very few steam trains stopped at Wool station and I knew the last one for Brighton was late afternoon. We decided to double-check every fault we had found. This was done, and the only thing we found was one tyre was a pound out of the required pressure. This was our last hope. Keeping our fingers crossed, we decided to go in. If there had been any more faults we knew we would have to wait until the next day to get away on our first leave. You can imagine the excitement when the examiner came out holding his thumbs up.

My worry now was McNeil. He had been put with another four. When we got back to the hut he was waiting for me. I understood they had not passed out very long before us. We made it to the station and caught the train all right. When we got into the carriage there was a Lance Corporal and a Sergeant who got into our same carriage. When the train started I sank back in the seat, breathless, as we had run from the camp the five miles to the station and I considered myself a good runner. I then undid the top button on my tunic. The Sergeant promptly ordered me to do it back up and gave us a lecture on how to behave in public when in uniform. Later, I got to know the Lance Corporal and the Sergeant very well. The Sergeant's name was Beech, and he lived in a village called Fletching, about eight miles from my home in Haywards Heath. The Lance Corporal lived in Newhaven and went on his own way at Brighton. On this journey back my thoughts kept going back to November and more so when we got out at Brighton, thinking about the Colour Sergeant when he marched me onto the station. Sergeant Beech travelled with us up to Haywards Heath and, while he had to wait for a bus, he was kind enough to buy McNeil and myself a drink in the Burrell Arms, which was opposite the railway station and bus stop. McNeil and I had a very enjoyable leave together, meeting and introducing McNeil to relations and friends.

37

Ben Westgate and his wife happened to call in to see my parents, not knowing I was home. I was very pleased to see him again. We chatted about our school days and our weekends at East Grinstead. McNeil was able to join in the conversation as he was very mechanically minded. As things turned out, it was to be the last time I would see Ben or his wife. McNeil and I spent one evening in the Star Hotel and the other evening in the Liverpool Arms, where my mother played the piano accordion. Our leave was only a long weekend. We were running short of money so I asked my mother if there was any from the allowance I had made. I was told that, as she tried to put a little by, my father would borrow it and had never paid it back. I never asked again and accepted the fact that I would never see any of the allowance. I could have stopped it or cut it down, but that would have meant my mother would have suffered.

Returning to Bovington, we were transferred to Lulworth for our gunnery course. Each one of a tank crew had to be interchangeable and partially trained to carry out each other's tasks, i.e. driver, gunner, wireless operator, tank commander. The course consisted of being able to strip and reassemble the main gun, a Vickers water-cooled machine gun, and small arms and firing these from a moving tank. We practised firing in the early stages from a rocking simulator. We fired at miniature moving targets with airgun pellets from both the main gun and the machine gun. We were then issued with a Colt 45 each with canvas belt and leg holster – I must have looked like a miniature John Wayne! The 45 was a very heavy revolver with a terrible kick when fired. We eventually changed over to 38s.

We then carried out firing from moving tanks, using live ammunition, at First World War tank wrecks. On completion of our gunnery course, after three weeks, we returned to Bovington for further training.

I was still involved with cross-country running, and by now Bovington to me was becoming more like a second home. I was really enjoying the army life, and I was also one hundred per cent fit. We had everything at the camp, cinema, NAAFI, shops and a church which we had to go to on Sunday mornings if in camp. I am not a religious man, but I enjoyed the Royal Tank Corps band when we were marching to church.

There were two public houses in Wool, if we had any money, but when we did go down we were always made welcome. Of course there were always the ones who, after a couple of drinks, were looking for trouble. The landlord would find out their names and report then to the camp office. They would then be put under charge and end up peeling potatoes for hours over at the cookhouse. They would also be banned from that public house. If they committed the same offence in any other pub in the area they could be sent to the glasshouse at Aldershot. I often wondered if that was where the Canadian went. Apart from a few odd ones, the camp had a good name. The glasshouse was like an army prison. Once in the gate you had to double-run most times with a pack on your back. No prisoners were ever allowed to walk. I am not giving the reader a picture of what life was like in the glasshouse from personal experience.

Many times on the parade ground Sergeant Voller warned us we were a hopeless shower but could improve after coming out of the glasshouse. In fact, we passed out for drilling with very high marks. Up to then we never knew Sergeant Voller was married, but because he was so pleased with us, that day he brought his wife and two children over from the married quarters to meet us. We were formed up outside our hut and Mrs Voller walked through the squad and congratulated each one of us. This was the very first time we realised Sergeant Voller was human after all the names we had been calling him. Before we left Bovington, he was promoted to Sergeant Major. At the end of the course we all respected him very much. It was some years later that I learnt that Sergeant Major Voller was killed during an air raid on Bovington.

We were due to leave Bovington in June 1939. During the last months, we were able to go on leave. We would put in for a pass, usually, in my case, for a long weekend. McNeil would come with me. He did get a long leave and went home to Scotland. He wanted me to go with him to meet his parents. He came from Glasgow, and I have often regretted that I did not go,

39

as things were to turn out. One weekend, when McNeil was in Scotland, I came home on a weekend leave. I had to report back into the guard room at 8 o'clock on the Monday morning. I had to catch the train from Haywards Heath. I cannot remember the exact time, but believe it to have been about 8 p.m. on the Sunday evening – and if Sergeant Beech was also up for the weekend, we would meet in the Burrell Arms about 7 p.m., that is the time the pubs opened then, and have a drink together before getting the train. I was never really sure if he would be there, as he sometimes came home on leave at a different time from me.

I was having a drink, and some friends came in and we were chatting and drinking because I was in uniform and just going back, and they would insist on me having one more before I left. Sergeant Beech did not come in. I wish he had. Having had quite a few drinks, I was not worrying about the time when I realised I had missed that train. I knew that was the last train to enable me to be back in camp by 8 a.m. on the Monday morning, so I would have to travel back on the Monday. I would then be put under charge for being absent without leave. This was a serious crime, and my first thoughts were of the glasshouse. The only thing I could do was to cycle. I said my goodbyes to my friends and told them I had no idea when I would see them again (if ever), ran home to Woodlands, got my old cycle and off I went. I had no idea how far it was, but having travelled the 272 road when I used to visit my sister in Bath, at least when I got to Salisbury it would not be difficult to find my way to Bovington.

I cycled through the night and was making, I thought, very good time until the beer I had drunk got the best of me and I fell off the cycle and went to sleep in the road. I don't know how long I was sleeping, but when I woke up it was just getting light. Off I went again when a lorry came along. This was the first transport I had seen all night. I stopped him and he put the cycle in the back of the lorry. He was going through Salisbury. I had remembered cycling through Winchester. He dropped me off at a road which would take me down to Blandford Forum. This he thought would be only about ten miles to the camp. I checked in the guard room at 8.30 a.m. Monday morning and was promptly put under charge to be in front of the Commanding Officer the following day.

That Monday most of the personnel in the camp were called out to fight the moors fires which were threatening the camp. I thought if the camp was destroyed by fire I would get off the hook – no such luck. I was marched in front of the officer the next day and the charge was read out. He asked me to reply to the charge. I told him the truth – that I had had too much to drink and had cycled from Haywards Heath to get back in camp. I don't think he believed me. I asked him that whatever happened to me could I please be allowed to take my cycle down to Wool station to put it on a train to send it home. He asked me, 'Where is this damned cycle you are talking about?' to which I replied it was round the back of the guard room. I had been told to leave it out of sight as it would make the place untidy. He ordered someone to go across to the guard room and bring the cycle over. I realised then he had not believed a word I had told him.

Back came the chap, who reported to the officer the cycle was now outside the office for him to see. I had this old cycle some years. It was very rusty, but nevertheless had served me well. He went to have a look at it. The charge was dismissed. He asked me if I had the money to send it back on the train. I said no, but one of my mates was going to lend me some until pay day. He instructed my Sergeant escort to take me over to the paymaster's offices and a travel warrant would be waiting for me to put the cycle on the next train to Haywards Heath and to arrange transport to take me down to the station with the cycle. He advised me not to have too much to drink at the last moment before returning from leave. He admired my efforts to get back. I never missed another train. The approximate distance from Haywards Heath to Bovington camp is 80 miles. I still keep in contact with Mick Pateman, who served with me at Bovington and now lives a few miles from me. When one tries to remember things 60 years ago, it helps to chat together. We still go back from time to time.

As I have mentioned, the news coming in was not good. We

were drawing towards a crisis as in 1938. Conscription was announced in April 1939 with the first call-up on 1 July 1939. More recruits were arriving at Bovington and training became more intense. More time was spent on the tank training grounds, as very soon there would be very large manoeuvres taking place on Salisbury plain.

We did not have many tanks at Bovington at this particular time, mainly Whippets and a few Crusaders. The Whippet was a very small tank, only six tons, with a crew of three: driver, gunner and commander, who operated the wireless, also he controlled the crew through intercom. When we went out training or on manoeuvres, we interchanged positions. There was a very peculiar fault on the Whippets: when they were being driven at speed, averaging about 30 mph on a good surface, the driver sat down on a very low seat with feet on the foot controls and each side of him a brake lever, which when pulled back put a brake hold on the sprocket wheel that engaged the track. For example, pull back on the right lever and the tank will turn right, pull back on the left lever and it will turn left. When the tank approached a speed of say 25–30 mph, it would change the brake levers over into reverse, i.e. pull back on the right lever and the tank would turn left and vice versa with the left one. There was no indication to the driver when at speed that it had changed over to what we used to call reverse steering. The only way was to gently hold onto the levers and feel for it. One had the same problem when speed was reduced and steering changed back to normal. I hope the reader will understand how I have tried to explain this and will, I am sure, wonder why I need to have explained it all. I can assure you, when you read on further, I had a very good reason. I have changed the names of the controls to make it more understandable. For example, the brake levers were called Rackems. All this only applied to the Whippet which we were using at that time. Later Whippets had this fault rectified.

Just prior to manoeuvres, we were crewed up to a particular tank. My position was gunner in a Whippet. The driver was a reservist recently called back up, by the name of Bill Meadows, and the tank commander was Second Lieutenant V. D. E. York.

42

There were other types of tanks taking part, but I was only ever involved with the Whippet and Cruiser. After this it was Cruisers throughout the rest of my service.

The manoeuvres were to take place for a few days and over a weekend. Although there was very little traffic on the roads in those days, there would be odd times when we would come off the moors and onto the public roads for short periods. Everything on the manoeuvres was carried out as it would be if ever we were on active service. We had our bedrolls to sleep in, corned beef better known as bully beef, army biscuits, everything for self-service, including a portable cooker. Eventually we were to find out there were seven ways of serving bully beef! Recipes can be supplied, please send SAE and a cheque for £100!

McNeil and myself were now told that, after the manoeuvres, we would be moving to Parham Down, which was a holding camp near Aldershot, to be kitted up with tropical clothes and gear and then embark for Egypt. Mick got his posting to Warminster.

The manoeuvres started early August 1939 on a Saturday morning. The Air Force were involved. I cannot remember details of what was going on, except that if any aircraft spotted us they would bomb our tanks with bags of flour. If a bag hit us we had to register a hit. After three hits we were considered knocked out. All was going well until tea time. We had been attacked several times, but no hits. Commander York ordered Bill to get off the moor and onto a hard road which could be seen about 50 yards away. We were travelling along by the side of the road. Bill moved over and onto the road. We then found ourselves going down a steep hill. On the right-hand side was a bank, and the tank was gathering up a fair speed when suddenly we shot up the bank and into the air, turning over three times, back on the road and finishing up upside down on our cupolas! There was no way of getting out. Bill had switched off the engine, thank goodness, as the petrol came pouring out from the tanks. We could hear a lot of shouting outside, warning people who had gathered round. We wondered where they had come from, as there were only a few houses and a pub. The

43

shouting was to warn people not to smoke. If we had caught fire, no one could have helped us. We could hear a lot of shovels at work. They were digging earth from the bank and covering the petrol on the road. They had piled it all around the tank, hoping if there was a fire outside it might stop it reaching the inside. There must have been some very quick thinking on the outside. We had sorted ourselves on the inside but had another problem; in the floor of the tank were several 12-volt wet batteries which were now upside down in our new ceiling. Sulphuric acid was dripping all over the inside. We asked for a tool to be passed inside through the driver's visor. We removed the plates, releasing the acid into a dixie, and emptied it down by our feet. This was better than the drips coming down all over the inside.

The recovery chaps had arrived and informed us it would be a few hours before the necessary gear would arrive to pull us upright. All we could do then was to sit and chat. Comm.York had not long been married and lived in Pinner in Harrow. Bill was married and lived in Worcester. I was not married. Bill had only returned a few days ago and since had been driving Crusaders. He had not been very well informed about the reverse steering on this particular tank. Bill was not put on charge over this. About 8 p.m. that evening the recovery pulled us upright. The tank was loaded on a recovery vehicle and taken back to be checked over. Comm.York went off to command another tank after medical checks, and Bill and myself were taken out of the manoeuvres. We had to be checked over by the medicals. Meantime, we were told to stay in the pub, where we would be collected and returned to camp. Most of the locals in the pub had been out helping with the earth moving. Bill and I were made very welcome, although we had no money we did have a few drinks, compliments of the landlord and locals. All we suffered was a few bruises.

With the manoeuvres over, those who were being posted to Egypt moved on to Parham Down. McNeil and myself kept together. For the first time we slept under canvas. For the short time we stayed at Parham we kept polished-up on Morse, parades and attending classes for education. I was still able to study for my first-class certificate.

44

At the end of August we were told embarkation would be delayed and all leave was cancelled. On 3 September war was declared. I remember thinking I had done the right thing after all, and now we were at war and I was fully trained. Within a few days we left Parham Down and went to Warminster, again under canvas in a bell tent. I cannot remember how many of us were in each tent. It was round with a pole in the centre, and we slept with our feet to the pole. There were arguments as to who slept near the flap opening because of the convenience to get out to use the toilet – more so after a few beers the night before. Mick Pateman was in the barracks. When he heard we had arrived, he came over to see me. He had passed out, as I had, as a driver/operator. Our posting to Egypt had gone out of the window. We now joined up with the Second Battalion, and we now had Cruiser tanks. We were formed into squadrons of 16 tanks in each squadron. Each consisted of four troops. Each troop was commanded by rank ranging from Sergeant upwards in rank to Captain. A Major would control the whole squadron. When it came to crews it surprised me when First Lieut. York, who was also posted to the Second Battalion, requested Bill Meadows as driver, myself as wireless operator and Bert Millar, who was another reservist, as gunner. From now on there would be no interchanging, only if anyone of the crew was not able to carry on. Without appearing rude, I shall refer to the crew by their nicknames, i.e. Yorkee, Bill and Dusty. I was called Justice. We carried out intensive training together, thinking we would soon be going over to France – how wrong we were.

Now that we had reached a satisfactory point in our training, crews could go on short leave, only one crew at a time. As McNeil was in another troop, it meant he would not be able to come home with me again. Sergeant Beech was a commander in our troop of four tanks. It was when our crew went on leave that I learnt that Dusty lived in Dorking, which is approximately 25 miles from Haywards Heath. We were no longer allowed to wear blues and had to be armed at all times. We wore khaki with the leg holster and a loaded Colt 45. This is how I had to go out for a drink.

I was home on leave, carrying a gas mask and wearing a leg

holster and a 45. If I was wearing civilian clothes and was pulled up by the army police I would be held on the local police station. If it was proved that I was in the armed forces I would be transported back to my unit, put under charge and, because this is a very serious offence, would be certain to go to the glasshouse. Military Police were experts at spotting a soldier in civilian clothes, haircut etc. Saturday evenings they would go round all the pubs in the area, looking for deserters now the war was on.

After this leave, we carried out more training in the Cruiser, which was about 30 tons with a top speed on the flat of 30 mph, armed with a two-pounder gun, one machine gun and two smoke ejectors fitted on the outside of the turret, and 200 gallons of petrol in two tanks. Inside the tank near the floor was a pipe with a tap coming from the petrol tanks. The floor of the tank was sloped so that, when the tap was opened, petrol would flood the whole tank. This was designed to destroy the tank when ignited. We carried 60 rounds of two-pounder shrapnel shells and 60 of armour-piercing rounds, several belts of machine gun ammunition and about 12 smoke bombs. All the two-pounder shells were in racks around the inside of the turret. The wireless was situated at the back of the turret at working height. A large canvas bag hung down the back of the gun to receive empty shell cases. The Cruiser drank one gallon of petrol to one mile on flat surfaces, on rough ground much more. I have explained this to the best of my memory.

Just before Christmas 1939, rumours were flying around that very soon we would be moving. There was no doubt in our minds it would be France. The rumours soon came true. We were ordered to pack up and prepare to move. I went over to the main block to say my goodbyes to Mick, and he told me they would soon be moving too. When I say pack up, this was any personal things into the tank. Bedrolls were packed into an iron basket which was fitted along the back of the tank. From now on the tank was to become our home, and we would sleep by it when on active service. We had to load the tanks on flats at the railway siding. Flats were long wooden floors on railway wheels. Two skids would be placed at the end of the flat and the

46

tank would be driven up the skids on to the flats, a very tricky operation for the drivers. Once loaded, we would chain it safe. When all 16 tanks were loaded, the crews reported to the motor pool to board the lorries in which they were to be transported. Our destinations were kept secret. We were wondering which port we would sail from. The column was led by staff cars carrying officers including our new Squadron Commander – Major Carlton. At the rear was the B echelon, which carried all supplies, i.e. cookhouse, petrol, ammunition and any other comforts that might be required.

It did not take us long to realise we were travelling north. Perhaps we were sailing from a port on the east coast. It was hard to believe when we arrived in Luton! We went into a hall that was to be our new dining room. It was now late evening when we all gathered in the dining room for a briefing by Major Carlton. We would be staying in civilian billets. The dining room would also be the place to parade. Mornings the tanks would be in the side streets around us. We would go to the station and collect our bedrolls etc. and be back for a meal in the dining room. After the meal we would be allotted our billet. Next morning after breakfast we would unload the tanks and bring them to their allotted position in a side street. After the meal, we were taken in batches to be put into our civilian billet. It was now very late at night. The sergeant major took our batch of about 30. He had a torch and a list, and at the first house he knocked on the door and when it opened he just said, 'One in here,' and so it went on. McNeil and myself hoped to get in together, as sometimes there were two or three going in. There were only a few of us left now, and all singles. At the next I went in. I was shown the bedroom, and as I was very tired I got my bedroll out on the floor.

The next morning I met the husband, Bert, and the landlady, whose name was Hilda, who told me her mother lived next door and, as it turned out, McNeil was in there with the mother. That evening, when I arrived back, I was asked why I had not used the bed. I explained that we were under strict orders not to sleep in the beds. She insisted that, if I wished to do so, I could. I took up the offer. I learnt later that the Third Battalion had moved up

47

from Warminster to Hitchin, but I never caught up with Mick again for many years. Luton was noted at that time for its ladies' hat factories which employed mainly women, and they greatly outnumbered the men. Now, with all our lot arriving in the heart of the town, this was the answer to a maiden's prayer. When the tanks left town for exercises, which was not often, really just to run the engines, we always had a lot of spectators, mainly women waving goodbyes, even though we might only be gone for two days.

Early in 1940, our crew was given leave. As I was on my own, I went down to Burgess Hill to Dot. We went out for a walk down to Wivelsfield, which is about two miles from Burgess Hill. I decided to visit my foster parents. I sensed everything was very different, as it was about 15 years since I last saw them. I must have appeared a very strange person dressed in khaki and wearing a holster with a 45 revolver. Also they could not understand why I had not visited them before. I explained about my father and was disappointed they had not enquired about me. We did not stop very long, and I never went back.

I went back to Luton. It was about three months after we arrived that we were on the move again. This time we left in our tanks. No one knew where we were going, but we knew it could not be far by going with tanks. In fact it was Dunstable, about eight miles away. We were all put into civilian billets again. I was on my own in a corner confectionery shop. They were very nice people, and I was given a very nice bedroom. Sometimes I was back early, and because of my experience in shop work returned their kindness by serving in the shop. While there I became ill with very bad flu. They contacted the squadron, who sent the medical officer down. He checked me over and decided to put me into a military hospital. They suggested to the officer that they would, with his permission, rather I stayed there if he would call to treat me. If I got any worse I would have to go to the hospital. After about three days I recovered and returned to duty.

All this time, since the war had started, very little had happened. In France it was now known as the Phoney War. Very soon we were on the move again. This time we loaded the tanks onto flats, so we knew we would be going on a long journey. We travelled in convoy to Ringwood in Dorset. We were fairly sure we would be heading for France. We were put into civilian billets for one night only. The next day we went to Southampton to take the tanks off the flats and load them onto a ship, which was also carrying tanks of the Third Battalion. I looked around for Mick, but could not find him. I came to learn after the war that Mick sailed from Dover to Calais. Later I was to learn they had fought for about four days and that Mick had been captured. He was a prisoner of war for five years in Poland, and when released by the Americans had to walk 500 miles to a port in France to get home.

It was early in the evening at Weymouth, while we were waiting to board the ship, that we were paraded on the dock-side. We knew by the strict discipline of that parade that some-one of importance would be inspecting us. It was King George VI and the Queen. The King was wearing riding breeches, brown boots and highly polished leggings, and my memory went back to Mr Kent, the carpenter in Gower Road!

5

French Campaign

My squadron sailed from Weymouth and landed at Cherbourg the next morning. Our tanks arrived at another port and we travelled along the coast and collected them. We then headed for Dunkirk. Very soon after we were bombed by Stuka dive bombers – and this time it was not bags of flour! As we drew nearer to Dunkirk the situation became very confused. There were French cavalry retreating with their horses and holding our column up. I received a message over the wireless, which I passed to Yorkee, telling us to get off the road and make our way through whatever. We received a map bearing to guide us on our way. At least we were on the move again, even if it meant going through gardens, farms or anything that was in our way. All the time the sky was white with German parachutes. We knew now by messages I was receiving that the Germans had broken through and we had been sent over as the last resort. It now got quite dark, and although we were still in contact by wireless, we realised we were on our own.

Yorkee decided we would stop for the night to get some rest. The noise of the guns had been getting nearer and nearer. We pulled into a wood and had something to eat. Yorkee decided we would do one hour guard each, and he took the first hour and manned the wireless. I took the next hour, sitting on top of the tank with earphones on, listening to messages being passed from one tank to another in our squadron. I will try and give you an idea of how our communications by wireless worked. Firstly all the 16 sets were tuned into a given frequency, which was changed from time to time only on the orders of the Squadron Commander. Our code sign was the same as the name of our tank, 'Bolton'. When communicating by speech, or as it was called RT, we had a maximum range of 13 miles. After that we changed over to Morse. The nearer the tanks were together, the louder and clearer became the speech. When I was sitting on top of the tank, the speech was very loud and clear, apart from all the gunfire going on around. I spoke to some of the other tanks and reckoned we were only one mile apart or even closer. Some of the other tanks were engaging the enemy, so we knew the Germans were quite near. However, we were quite confident that we would join up at daylight. At last my hour came to an end and I was pleased I was going to get some more sleep.

Dusty took over from me. He hated operating the wireless. It must be remembered that Bill and Dusty were old reservists and only went back to Bovington for two weeks every year for refresher courses, and this was a rare time they would have to use the wireless. I lay down in the small ditch I had laid in before on my previous hour and went to sleep. Something woke me up. It was raining hard and water was running down the ditch all around me, but I was so tired I turned over and went to sleep again, but not for very long. I cannot remember who woke me up with their finger over their mouth, indicating to me not to speak, as I slowly got up soaked in ditch-water. I could hear a lot of voices coming from the wood and knew they were Germans. Yorkee beckoned us to go with him to the tank. We took our positions in it and closed the cupolas as quietly as we could. Yorkee passed me a message to send to the commander, informing him of our position. We were told to wait for further orders. It was not long before the message came back to destroy the tank, get out of the wood and make our way to Calais to be evacuated. We never realised things were as bad as that. We packed a few personal things into our haversacks, in my case tins of bully, biscuits, washing and shaving gear, socks and of course packets of Woodbine cigarettes. I always kept a good supply by the side of the wireless set.

I sent my last message that Bolton was closing down.

Outside there were a lot more German voices. We felt the whole wood was being taken over. Bill opened the petrol tap, Yorkee would fire a flare and set the tank on fire. We drew our revolvers and all left together, to get out of the wood as quickly as we could. Just before Yorkee fired the flare, Bill asked if I had taken the watch from the front of the wireless. I jumped up on the tank by the side of Yorkee, bent over and lifted the watch out of its pocket. It's hard to describe the next few minutes, when the tank went up with flames shooting up in the air. The Germans must have been in utter confusion as to what was happening. As we got further away, we could hear the ammunition exploding. At last we got out of the wood without any trouble. It was now breaking dawn and we rested for a while. It got light enough for Yorkee to study his map, and also it was now light enough to know where east was. We set off through some fields, hoping we were heading north. We soon came to a road on which there was a great number of French evacuees and French soldiers, and very soon we saw a few English soldiers who gave us our first update as to what was going on. There had been a large evacuation of troops from Dunkirk. They, like ourselves, were heading for Calais. At least we now knew we were on the right road. As we carried on the road it became more congested with French evacuees with all their belongings. All the time we could hear gunfire, which seemed to get louder as we got nearer to Calais. We were living on our bully and biscuits and sleeping in woods at night. At times the French would give us some food and hot drinks. I cannot remember how many days we had been going towards Calais, when we heard the bad news that it had fallen. Because of the congestion on the roads it was decided, between ourselves, to head across country, hopefully to get to another port before the Germans.

The roads were being machine-gunned by Stukas most of the day. The other problem now was that the Germans were infiltrating into France, dressed as English soldiers or officers and speaking good English. This made the French very suspicious of us. At one French farmhouse we asked for some water to shave and clean up and they invited us in, let us wash and shave and gave us a very good hot meal. The farmer and his wife spoke very good English. We were all chatting with each other over the meal and a few glasses of wine. After the meal the farmer told us he was willing to help us further by giving us a lift. He would take us to a certain point east of the River Seine and from then on we should be able to get to Le Havre, without too much trouble, in about three days. His wife had packed food and a bottle of wine each. He had a small van to take us in on the journey. He told us his wife and he were very suspicious of us at first, but after the meal were quite happy that we were English. He dropped us off and directed us as to the route to take. We said our goodbyes, and he set off on his return journey. For this man to take us as far as he did, and give us all the help he had, and to leave his family in order to take us down to the river at a time when he knew the Germans were coming through fast, showed great courage. We felt sure he was with the French Resistance and that others must have been helping in the background looking after his family. We felt the Germans must be so far back that our problems were over. The Stukas never gave up machine-gunning the refugees. The day after the farmer had dropped us, we heard gunfire in the distance. This became louder each day.

We went up a lane off the main road. Yorkee had worked the route out on his map and we should save a few miles to the port. Some way up this lane we came across a French tank. After checking everything, we could not find any reason why it had been abandoned. We stood back while Bill started it up in case there was a booby trap. The guns appeared to be OK, plenty of petrol, so off we went.

It was better than walking. We got back on the road. We were stopped by a French army officer who spoke fair English. He was surprised we were English driving a French tank. Anyway, he told us it was no good trying to get to Le Havre. We were suspicious about this officer, as there were parachutists dropping to the west of us. The way we were heading there was a bridge going over the Seine. It turned out he was organising a rearguard action to try and hold the Germans from using the bridge. I cannot remember at just what point this was on the Seine. When we got to the bridge, we were surprised to see how

53

many English and French soldiers were there. They had mined the bridge. The French officer came along with more stragglers he had collected. Now Yorkee was helping to organise the rearguard, we went across the bridge and found a good position, fired a couple of rounds up into the air as a check of the gun and waited. Most of the refugees managed to get across before the bridge was blown up.

The Germans came in from the east with lorries and infantry. They got to the river and we were firing at the lorries. I was surprised how much firing there was from our side and quite a lot of damage being inflicted on them. They must have been prepared for a rearguard and the bridge to be blown. They brought up several tanks to return fire. The next thing they were launching pontoon boats filled with infantry. Most of the rearguard were now retreating on foot. Yorkee gave the order to Bill to turn around and get moving. We headed away west. It would take the Germans some time to build a temporary bridge and to get their tanks across. That French officer had done a good job.

The next port we would head for was where we had started from – Cherbourg. At last we ran out of petrol, and as there were not many rounds left, we abandoned the tank in a wood, destroying it as much as we could. Off we set on foot again. It must be remembered, we had started our retreat believing it would only be a few days before we were evacuated. Now we were going into weeks. We were scrounging food or supplying ourselves from shops which had been deserted. I had about three pairs of socks which I washed in streams and laid them over the outside of my haversack to dry as we walked. I found this was important, to be able to change my socks as often as possible. We might not shave for days, but when we did it refreshed us to go on. Over the next few days we managed to get lifts, making good progress towards Cherbourg.

One morning, after sleeping in a wood (woods became our bedroom), we got back onto a road. A Frenchman who was with the refugees saw us in uniform. He was shouting as he came towards us. I happened to be in front when I saw he had a chopper in his hand. As he got nearer to me he raised it in the air. I could not understand what he was saying. Yorkee was shouting back to him in what French he knew. I pulled my revolver and aimed at him, and if he had not stopped would have fired. Some of the other French people got him settled down. He thought we were Germans. A few of the French were not very friendly towards us, and others were very helpful indeed.

I could never understand why they brought so much with them – handcarts, prams, anything on wheels loaded up. It caused so much congestion on the roads. The Stukas were gunning the roads every day. I saw many killed because they could not get off the roads in time. Whenever we managed to get a lift, it was slow going to get by all this congestion. We were between two fires, as the Stukas shot up lorries or transport. Although Dunkirk was about three weeks ago, they must have suspected that quite a few troops were still on the run.

Bill, Dusty and myself were always joking. I never heard anyone disheartened. Dusty could not understand why Yorkee always had the map upside down when he read it. There was never a dull moment. It's impossible to remember things that happened every day – only the highlights. One morning we were on the road which would take us up to Cherbourg. In fact, we were not many days away, there was one thing that we could not understand, there were no refugees. As we came round a bend in the road we could see a soldier at a crossroads with his arms up, directing the traffic. Someone said, 'Thank goodness for that, it's our Military Police.' Yorkee still had his binoculars, and he got them out to get a closer look, and as he was putting them back in his casual way said, 'It's a Military Police – the only thing wrong – he's a German.' It was back off the road again. We were fairly sure now that Cherbourg was cut off or had fallen. That crossroads traffic was travelling east to west and Cherbourg was north, so it was obvious to us what had happened. The one thing we did notice was that there was very little gunfire – some days none at all.

We knew our last hope was Brest, and looking at the map, it was a long way off. It was decided that, as we had come so far, we would carry on, but keep away from the main roads. After several days through fields, farms and woods, we decided to get on the road again if all was well. When we got on the road, there were no refugees or Germans. An army truck came along and gave us a lift. He was heading for Brest. We thought this was the end of our walking, but this was not to be. He had plenty of petrol, which would have taken us right in, but a half shaft broke and that was the end of our ride. The driver and his mate were now with us. After about a week, we were five miles from the port, where many seemed to be converging. There were all kinds of stragglers. Everyone was very exhausted. We were taking a rest before going on, and we were sitting on the roadside bank. I was changing my socks, Yorkee was walking up the road talking to two other officers and a sergeant who had a hailer – I can't imagine where he got that from.

The German planes were using more bombs, the noise was very bad. The sergeant then used his hailer. I cannot remember what his words were, but he was saying he would like everyone who could to form up in the road in a column of three, and we would walk into the docks at Brest in some kind of order. He was not going to march us but to walk at a fairly quick pace. The officers walked in front and the sergeant by the side of the column.

The column could have numbered anything from 100 to 200. The German planes were increasing in number as we got in nearer to the port. About three miles out, there were fields and fields of brand new British army vehicles of all kinds – lorries, staff cars, motorcycles, it was unbelievable – on both sides of the road. The planes were not bothering to bomb or destroy any of them. We knew now the Germans were not far behind us. Some of the chaps were getting on motorcycles, hoping there was enough petrol to get the final few miles. The guards on these vehicles gave up. The sergeant stopped our column to ask for volunteers who would stay to destroy them, only reservists were required, no regulars, so that let me out. Dusty volunteered, and we shook hands and left him and some others behind. This was the first time our tank crew had broken up. Bill was saying Dusty was mad. I said it was his own choice.

There was a shop that must have been a general stores. The owner was giving away anything one wanted. I had a bottle of champagne, which I put in my haversack with my socks round it and some cigs. It was about noon and a very nice warm summer's day when our column arrived outside the docks. The first sight I got, across the other side of the docks, about 200 yards away, was a very large troop ship, greyish in colour. A large number of chaps were running along the end of the docks to get round the other side of the ship. The Stukas were concentrating on this ship. I noticed the ship was crammed with soldiers around all the decks. I could not see any space at all. As I was looking at it and contemplating my next move, a Stuka dived down. I thought he was going to crash onto the ship, but he pulled out and dropped his bombs. One of those I saw go straight down the funnel. There was a terrible explosion far above all the bombing and gunfire going on around us. The ship went straight down in a matter of two minutes.

At this moment I noticed a small vessel coming into the dock where I was standing. The skipper, in a Scottish accent, was shouting to us to jump when he was close enough to the side. I glanced back to where the troop ship had been. All I could see was men running back round the end of the dock, making for our side. As the vessel got into the side, I, with others, jumped onto a tarpaulin. When there were about 30 of us, the skipper shouted no more and pulled back, turned and headed out to sea. It was terrible to leave so many chaps behind. One soldier had a machine gun on board and was firing at the planes. As we were looking back, someone shouted that the flag flying over the city had been lowered and the German flag had been hoisted.

As we were heading out to sea we passed another couple of small boats going in, but we felt sure the Germans would have been down on the docks by then. Our skipper was trying to warn them to turn round, but they did not hear him. Hopefully they would see the German flag.

As we got out into the open sea, the skipper was telling us he had bought his collier down from the north loaded with coal for Southampton, but before he could dock had received a message to go to Brest to pick up the 'stragglers', as we were called. He thought, as many people think now, that all the troops had been pulled out from Dunkirk and that was the end of it. But a lot of the stragglers had been landed at other ports in France. There were only a few of us who had trekked from Dunkirk to Brest, which could have been in the region of 800 miles, in about five weeks. Someone must have made a terrible mistake allowing thousands of new vehicles to be shipped into France. They were never used or recovered and maybe even landed in Brest after the Dunkirk evacuation.

Our collier was well down in the water. We slept one or two nights on the boat and were to land at Avonmouth early one morning. Unfortunately, because of the weight with the extra troops on board, the collier grounded. The skipper made contact with the shore, and it was arranged for some small boats to come out and get us off. The first small boat arrived, and the first person on board our collier was a Customs and Excise man. As he was searching us, he was receiving a lot of abuse and swearing. However he let me off with my bottle of champagne. I told him he was welcome to my socks. I believe that when he realised where we had come from, he was very embarrassed. We were taken off by the small boats after thanking the skipper for what he had done and saying our goodbyes. After a clean-up and a meal, Bill and myself were transported to rejoin our own unit. We arrived at camp near Southampton and were put under canvas.

During my research I discovered the troop ship in Brest harbour had several thousand troops on board when it sank. This occurred on 19 June 1940, the day the Germans occupied the city. I have often wondered why all the thousands of troops left in France after Dunkirk were without any air support and left to their own devices.

6

North African Campaign

Most of our squadron was at Southampton, and it was here I was told my friend McNeil had been killed when his tank was knocked out at Dunkirk. It occurred at the time when I was told on the wireless that some of our tanks were in action. Yorkee had got back, and we met him later that day. Dusty arrived back. Now we were a complete tank crew without a tank. The squadron was given a lecture by Major Carlton. We would be at this camp for the next few weeks. During that time he would be bringing in a physical training instructor to get us to look like soldiers again.

One thing I have forgotten to tell you about Major Carlton, he had a very bad stutter when addressing the squadron, but I never heard him stutter when speaking over the wireless.

We had been allotted new tanks which were Cruisers, and they arrived that day. Although they were new, everything had to be checked over by the crew and, after carrying out short exercises, Bolton II was given the OK. Then we could have a short leave, as usual, one crew member at a time. The leave was allotted so some crews would not always get weekends. The next day a sergeant physical training instructor gave us an hour of really hard physical exercises, which were carried out in a field. The weather was very warm. During the hour I was sure I knew the sergeant from sometime before the war. When the hour was finished, I asked him if he was George Martwick from London Lane in Cuckfield. When I asked this, he recognised me. He had to go on to another class but told me he was giving

59

us another hour that afternoon and would have a chat after that. His father worked for the Scottish contractors in Carter's gang, the same as myself. George knew my brother quite well. He was an amateur boxer and, with my brother who was also a boxer, hired a room over the Heath Hotel in Haywards Heath on Sunday mornings to train themselves and others. We had several chats together. We were certainly very fit again once he had finished the course. We said our goodbyes and I have never heard anything of the family again, even though they only lived two miles from my home.

When I went home on a short leave everyone was sad to hear about McNeil, but we had a party anyway. Dot came to see me. We opened the bottle of champagne and I asked my parents to look after the watch. It was a very short leave, only two days, as we were going to be on the move again. Back at camp things were moving very fast. One day the whole squadron had to parade in front of their tanks. Major Carlton inspected us. When he had finished we saw a staff car arrive. Major Carlton went to receive the passenger. It was the Prime Minister, Winston Churchill, with Mrs Churchill, who then inspected each tank crew and wished us luck and off he went, puffing his cigar.

It was expected that the Germans would now invade England at any time, and we thought all the rush to prepare us was because of the expected invasion. Because of this it came as a complete surprise when we were ordered to collect our tropical gear and were given inoculations. The next move was to put the tanks on the flats at the railway station.

We travelled by a different train and eventually arrived in Liverpool. The tanks had already arrived so we unloaded them and drove to the docks, where they were loaded onto a ship which was to carry all the tanks, lorries, staff cars, motorcycles, armoured cars, in fact anything with tracks or wheels.

We now carried a haversack and kitbag. We were loaded up in a very large troopship which had been converted from a luxury liner, I never got to know the name. Bill, Dusty, myself and one other chap had a cabin which we could not complain about. We lay at anchor overnight and sailed out of the Mersey early the next morning. We were paraded on deck and given lifeboat drill and spent a lot of time exploring the ship. As we got more out to sea it was becoming very rough. A lot of the chaps were being sick. We were amazed how many ships were joining us in convoy including navy ships, destroyers, etc. As we got to know later, it was the largest convoy that ever sailed out of Liverpool. We were given a lecture informing us we were going to Egypt (there had been rumours), and all of the do's and don'ts when serving in a foreign country (for sure we had heard all this before). The next morning many of the chaps were still being sick..We had breakfast – kippers – and after this nearly everyone was sick! I have been lucky and never suffered from sea sickness. We still had to carry out certain duties on the ship, but had a lot more free time, which was spent playing games, cards and a game which most chaps like myself had not heard of or played before; it was Housey-Housey. This became the main game and was the forerunner to today's bingo.

We stopped at Gibraltar, I believe it was to take on supplies, and then sailed on. It was here that we realised we were not going through the Mediterranean but around Africa via the Cape of Good Hope, up and past Madagascar, through the Red Sea and Suez Canal to Alexandria.

The German submarines, known as U-boats, became more active as we went further south down the west coast of Africa, and several of the smaller ships were sunk. We anchored off Freetown on the west coast and on the Equator. Small boats came out to our ship and when you threw pennies into the sea the occupants would dive off their boat and would recover them. There must have been hundreds of pennies thrown over at the same time, and they recovered every one. It was very hot and while there, we had an electrical storm. This was the first time I had the experience of a storm like this without a cloud in the sky. It was quite frightening. There was no wind, not even a breeze, when this storm struck. There was very little thunder but terrific fork lightning. Every flash seemed to be aimed at me personally, but all the chaps felt the same way as I did. None of us had experienced anything like this, as most of us had not been out of England before. As we sailed out of Freetown the little boats followed for a time, the people still diving for pennies. We sailed on down the coast with a calm sea. We had only had that rough sea the first day or two, and since then it had been very calm. We docked in Cape Town only for an afternoon and evening. We proceeded on and docked again in Durban, where we took on supplies. We travelled on without any incident, in fact we were now looking forward to getting on to dry land again.

It became more interesting when we got into the Red Sea. On entering the Suez Canal, our ship seemed to only just fit the width of the canal. I cannot remember if we had tugs pulling us all the way or only part of the way. It was our first sight of Egyptians in their strange clothes. We had now changed into tropical gear as it was very hot. The canal opened up quite wide at one point to allow the smaller ships to pass us. At last we docked at Alexandria. We had been on the ship for six weeks. We were transported to a place called El Amiriya, about 16 miles out of Alexandria. There we were under canvas, ridge tents, not bell tents, this time. We were told to rest, as we would be up that night working. All qualified drivers had to parade early that night. We were taken in lorries back to the docks. The ship carrying all the army vehicles was unloading. We took our turn, when a vehicle was lowered by crane from the ship, to drive it away out to El Amiriya. Then we were transported back to the ship to receive another vehicle. This went on all night. It could be any type of vehicle, tank, motorcycle etc. It was while I was waiting my turn in the dock in the moonlight that I recognised a chap sitting on a bale next to me. He was with the Third Battalion of RTR, and his name was Dick Stammer, from Kents Road in Haywards Heath. We went to the Council school at the same time, and I knew his sister quite well! I heard Dick was killed in action a few days after arriving in the desert.

There was a single railway track which ran from a point near El Amiriya up to Mersa Matruh, where it terminated on the edge of the Western Desert. Shortly after arriving at El Amiriya, we loaded the tanks on flats at the railway and started our journey. We had to sleep at night by our tank on the flat. This was the first time that I found out that the desert was such a very cold place at night. I cannot remember how long the journey took, but I believe we slept for two nights. We reached the end of the track and unloaded. We set off for our first taste of the desert. There was only one hard road, which was the coast road running from Egypt through to Libya to Tunisia. From this hard road were a few tracks south down into the desert. It was very sandy, rocky terrain. Further south it was sand only. We formed our first leaguer with the tanks in a circle. One of the first jobs we learnt to do when arriving at any leaguer area was toilets. Each member of the crew would walk out a reasonable distance from the tank in different directions and make a hole as deep as possible. This now became one's own personal toilet called 'Prairie Rose'. Our B echelon would arrive to replenish the tanks with petrol, ammunition and hopefully a hot meal, which was always hot soup, for us. About the middle of September 1940, the Italians, who occupied all of Libya, had crossed into the Egyptian side and now occupied Sidi Barrani. We were the first tanks along with other battalions to be operating in the Western Desert. We were formed into the 7th Armoured Division, known as the Desert Rats. We were under the command of General Wavell. We took over the positions of the Hussars who, with armoured cars, were intercepting Italian columns bringing supplies in from Tobruk to camps around 60 miles down in the desert.

The first enemies we encountered in the desert were the snakes and scorpions. We always laid a black groundsheet down on the sand to rest on. We could always see if any snakes or scorpions came on it. Each of the tank crew had to do two hours guard duty on the tank, and because it never got very dark, could keep watch on the groundsheet. Bill was the only one who was stung by a black scorpion, early one morning. He was quite ill for about three days. We now handed in our Colt 45s and were given 38s. These were very much lighter.

About 60 miles south of Tobruk was the largest of the Italian camps, named Nibeiwa. One day it was reported that a large column of Italians with supplies was about halfway down in the desert between Tobruk and Nibeiwa, and we were ordered to intercept and destroy it. We had Scottish infantry supporting the attack. The column had stopped and was having a meal. They had tank support, but we were far superior with our tanks. We had traversing turrets and they had fixed turrets, so the driver had to manoeuvre to line the gun onto a target. By running round them they were bound to shed a track as they tried to fire at us, and then they were sitting ducks. Their tanks were soon destroyed and we went into their leaguer area. Our cupolas were open, and I heard a strange noise above all the noise of the guns. When I looked out of the top we had just gone through their cookhouse, and it was the noise of tin cans and cooking stoves as we crushed them. Anyway, they gave up and we withdrew, leaving it to the infantry to sort out. We heard there were several hundred prisoners taken, and that was only classed as a small patrol action.

The supply columns which came down from Tobruk after losing the large one were smaller but more numerous. We spent the next two months intercepting supply lines. Sometimes we would go across the border twice a day, wiping up small columns. It was during one of these patrols, as we were using our main gun on some Italian tanks, that the first shell case to be ejected, wedged itself across the top inside of the bag which received the used shell cases. It would have been impossible to let them pile up on a small floor space. We could have been in trouble with the traversing turret jamming or, as they are very hot when ejected, in trouble because of fire. Our cupola lids were open, so I decided to catch them as they were ejected and throw them out through the lids. When the case in the bag had cooled, I was able to remove it. The cordite fumes were very intense when we were in action, another reason to leave the tops open.

The next morning I had blisters over the inside of my hands and I found it was very painful to touch anything. The medical officer would come into our leaguer that morning when he was on his rounds visiting the squadrons. Yorkee ordered me to see him. I was hoping I might get a few days leave in Alex. No such luck. When I saw the officer, he called over two chaps from a tank crew nearby to hold me standing up. He then cut the blisters with his scalpel, releasing the fluid. When they let me go, I was running around in the sand calling him all the rotten bastards I could think of. I soon recovered and apologised to the officer. He assured me I would not have any more trouble with them. Later that same day we were again in action. During these many patrol actions I very often wondered when I saw the sun rise over the horizon if I would be around to see it set that evening. I discovered many other chaps had the same thoughts.

During the days when we were left in peace, we carried out maintenance on the tank. We would be split up because Italian planes were forever over us, bombing and machine-gunning. Some days we were on our own and could not see any of the other tanks, but were in wireless contact. I had a small speaker which I connected to the set and had it outside the tank, which relieved me of having headphones on all the time, as the temperature at midday could be 110 degrees F. It was no fun sitting on top of the tank. As we were south of the coast we sometimes came across a camel train. This would be about seven camels with maybe two or three families of Bedouins, travelling from Cairo to Tripoli, with dogs, chickens and everything they needed to live on. When we came across them they would trade eggs for our bully beef. The eggs were very welcome, as we were living mainly on bully and biscuits and hot soup when B Echelon arrived with our supplies. The Bedouin were always very friendly. Sometimes we would find a camel train that had been shot up by Italian aircraft. On two or three occasions we came upon a shot-up train, and the vultures and rats were still feeding on the bodies of the Bedouins and camels. It must have been obvious to the Italian pilots that these were innocent camel trains.

During the day we kept ourselves covered up as much as possible against the heat. During sand storms we wore goggles. The wind during these storms was very ferocious and difficult to walk against. We could lean over at an angle of 45 degrees and lie on the wind. When the storm was over, the whole landscape would be altered.

During one of our rests, the tanks were in open leaguer. This means the tanks were out in a very large circle, in fact sometimes you could not see the tanks on each side. Now the most stupid thing one can do in the desert is to wander away from your tank without keeping it in sight. You could turn round and, if you could not see it, you were lost. Several chaps were lost through wandering too far and losing their sense of direction. On this particular rest, we had cleaned our guns and carried out what maintenance we had to do. Bill was still doing some jobs on the Meadows' V8 engine. There was a trail of large ants going by our tank, so Dusty and myself started to walk to see where they were going to. There were two columns going one way and two columns going the other way. We followed the trails for some distance but, as there was no end, we decided to turn round and go back to the tank. When we turned round we could not see the tank. We had not realised we had walked up a sand dune and down the other side. It was the most horrible feeling I have ever experienced, looking round and seeing only sand. We kept our fingers crossed and decided to follow the ant trail back. This worked out and we safely returned to the fold. Perhaps David Attenborough would have the answer to the ant trail, but we could have lost our lives in an unpleasant way trying to find out.

As the sun set it would become very cold. The shorts we wore during the day could be unbuttoned and let down at night. As the sun rose in the morning we could button them back up. We were becoming more desperate for spares for the tank. The batteries were not holding their charge. Bill was having clutch trouble, and other minor things we needed. The rest of the tanks in the squadron were having the same problems. Yorkee now had to go back to Alex. He was suffering from piles and needed an operation. We had a replacement commander while he was away. One morning, when we were on our own, we had a visit from General Wavell. He asked if everything was OK, and we asked when we could expect the spares we required, but we did not get a direct reply. About two weeks after Yorkee had left a light tank pulled up by our tank, with Yorkee driving it on his own (no crew). He had had the operation and had discharged himself and come up on the railway with the light tank which was required by another squadron. We had to help him out of the driving seat, which was a pool of blood. He was still bleeding very badly but insisted he was taking his position as commander of our tank. As it was, he soon recovered (we always suspected he was mad!). Having said that, Yorkee was a very respected officer in our squadron. He never wanted to miss any actions. Our crew had kept together and I am sure he had heard about a big push against the Italians called 'Compass', which was to start early December 1940, hence his reason for discharging himself.

We carried out many patrol actions up until November 1940. After being in the desert three months, we were given one week's leave. Yorkee went with another officer, a Captain Williamson. Bill, Dusty and myself went back to Alex, and decided to go down to Cairo for a few days. We stayed in Alex for two nights. We met a Navy chap who invited us to the fleet club in Alex in the evening, as they had a big Housey-Housey, paying out £50 a game. We had tried to clean up the best we could, as our faces were covered in blackheads, caused through heat and lack of water for washing and shaving, and still looked a bit of a mess. By having electrical massage for about half an hour at a time for three days, they were completely cured. The treatment was carried out at the barbers with the usual argument of how much to pay.

We went to the club and were having a drink when we heard a row going on between some Australians. Within a short time the whole club was invaded by more Australians, fighting with chairs, bottles and anything they could lay their hands on. We got under the table and stayed there. Very soon ambulances were taking the injured away. When we got out the whole place had been wrecked. It was the first lot of Australians that had arrived in Egypt, and they were mainly hobos who had been conscripted into the army. In Alex and Cairo there were certain brothel streets which came under the control of the British military authority, and any other brothel areas were out of bounds. These Australians went mad and wrecked a whole street in Cairo. I believe the name of the street was Birka. They smashed in doors and threw beds out through windows onto the streets. Our own military police, who were hardnuts, could not control them. I heard the trouble started because they would not wait their turn. Mussolini, in a broadcast which I heard myself,

67

informed the Egyptians that he would not bother to bomb Alex or Cairo as the Australians were wrecking both cities for him – that was how bad they were! The Australians who followed into Egypt later could not do enough to make up for what the first lot had done.

We caught a train down to Cairo, which in itself was quite an experience. We booked into a bed and breakfast hotel just on the outskirts called Heliopolis. From our hotel we could catch a tram down into the city. We had the same driver each morning who let us take it in turns to drive the tram. We went to have electrical treatment on our faces, and after a while began to look like human beings again. We went out to the pyramids and took a tour through the inside. About halfway in, as there was no lighting inside, the guide had a kind of flare which went out. He wanted us to pay him for another flare before we went on. This we refused to do and he began to get very nasty when we picked him up and threatened to throw him into one of the burial chambers. He lit another flare very quickly and we finished the tour without any further trouble.

The flies were quite a nuisance. Back in Cairo, we visited the well-known places such as the Blue Mosque, but Cairo was not my cup of tea. We travelled back to Alex and were invited onto an aircraft carrier, which was in for a short spell and had a reputation for its doughnuts! We had tea on board and were shown round some of the ship. They had a museum of pistols and would be willing to buy any we could get hold of.

We travelled up to El Amiriya and there we got a lift on the Mersa Matruh express and managed to rejoin our squadron without any problems. For a while we carried out our patrol interceptions of the Italian supplies. We were informed that a large attack was to be made on 9 December, and this was to be called codename 'Compass'. Early one morning, before daylight, we went through the wire which served as a border line and headed south down into the desert. We then went back up to come in the opposite way than would be expected by the Italians in Nibeiwa camp.

We had a sharp battle with their tanks, and within a short time Nibeiwa surrendered. There were thousands of prisoners taken, who were on the point of starvation, which proved our patrol interceptions had served their purpose. They were formed into columns and directed to walk into Egypt. The advance was being held up on the front all along the coast by so many prisoners.

Our tank, like many of the other tanks, was desperate for spares. After the battle for Nibeiwa, we had to be started by another tank with a tow chain. We were ordered to head north to Bugbug.

The only way we could travel in the desert was by compass bearings. We had a compass set in an insulated pocket in the floor of the tank so that it was not affected by metal. The commander could work out bearings and instruct the driver so as to keep on course. It may have taken us a day or two to reach Bugbug. We would leaguer over night and B echelon would replenish any supplies we needed – plus the hot soup!

Bill was still having trouble with the clutch slipping. He emptied a fire extinguisher and filled it with petrol and sprayed this into the clutch, which helped it to bite for a while. Also, we were having trouble with track pins breaking, and it was not easy getting a track back on in the desert.

The Italian planes were attacking us most days but did not do a lot of damage as the tanks always kept a good distance apart, thereby making a smaller target. Bugbug lies on top of an escarpment and when we arrived, we took positions in a line abreast at the bottom We came under heavy artillery fire while awaiting for the order to advance. This was the moment in which I felt fear, and I am sure it was the same for many others. Waiting for the order to advance gave us time to think, wondering what could happen. Sometimes these waits could be longer than others, maybe half an hour or more. There was never any talk of being taken prisoner, wounded or killed. On the contrary, talk would be about when it was all over, of returning to a normal life. It was always a relief when the order was given over the wireless to advance. After this the wireless sets were left on but no messages were passed until the silence was broken by Major Carlton. Once we moved, all was well as we had no more time to think.

The engine stopped on our tank and I wirelessed for another tank to get a tow line on. Dusty and myself got out and fixed the chain. The one thing the Italians were very good with was their artillery. Because two tanks were sitting together, we made a very good target. Bill was sitting waiting with the tank in gear. As we got the order to advance they dropped a shell at the back of our tank. The back lifted, the explosion jolted the tank forward and the engine started – the explosion had jump-started it. We got out, took the chain off and proceeded up the escarpment. Bill was doing a good job to keep the engine going. Just before we entered Bugbug, Yorkee shouted to me that there was an Italian on the back of our tank and he was drawing his revolver. I drew mine and looked out of the cupola. The Italian was lying on the back of the tank behind the turret. We both fired together and he rolled off. As we discovered after, he was trying to get a hand grenade between the covers of the petrol tanks. He could not see or realise that our cupolas were opened. All he would have needed to do was to drop it inside. We had seen many tanks hit with their cupolas jammed and the tank on fire and nothing could be done for them. This was the reason we kept ours open. When we entered Bugbug, there were so many Italians waving anything white. Indian infantry were rounding them up. While we were taking a rest there, Yorkee picked up an English rifle and plenty of ammunition. He hung the rifle over the smoke canister on the outside of the turret. We heard Bardia and Tobruk had fallen and the Italians were moving back.

We were then ordered to Fort Mechili, which was south of Tobruk. By now the number of tanks in our squadron was reduced, either knocked out or needing spares. We managed to carry on all the time we could get a tow. We arrived at the fort and sat a fair distance out, again coming under artillery fire from the fort defences. Another tank had us on the tow chain ready to move. I was amazed looking at that fort. Up to now I had only seen a fort like it in Beau Geste films. Yorkee lent me his binoculars to have a look, and I remarked to him that those walls must be very thick – I was thinking of our tank bouncing off the wall. The order came to advance and the tow chain

70

broke. Yorkee, not wanting to be left out of the action, jumped out and took command of the tank that was going to start us, and their commander came and took over ours. I had a surprise when I saw that it was Sergeant Beech. We were under very heavy artillery fire, and with the others moving we were a sitting duck. Sergeant Beech remarked to me that, when we got back to Haywards Heath, we would have a drink together in the Burrell Arms; I said I wouldn't say no to one now. We were receiving near misses and the tank was lurching with some of the explosions outside. Soon the firing stopped and we knew Fort Mechili had fallen. Yorkee arrived back and Sergeant Beech rejoined his tank. Our tank had been so badly damaged it was no longer able to operate. The damage was caused by very near misses, so close in fact that it had blown our bogey wheels off. We had felt the tank rock violently from time to time, and were amazed when we got out to see how much damage had been inflicted on us. It would be picked up by a tank carrier and be returned for repairs. If it had been considered not repairable it would have been set on fire and left. We took over another Cruiser from our troop. They in turn would soon be taking over another from the repair shop by carrier. The Cruiser we took over became Bolton III. The Italians were now in retreat.

It was now January 1941, and we had made our way back up to the coast road and were heading for Derna, which was an Italian seaplane base. Before we got anywhere near, we were ordered to a point on the escarpment, at the bottom of which was an Italian landing strip. From our position at the top we could see the runway, although there was a very bad sandstorm just at this time. We saw an Italian plane come in and land. Yorkee decided that out of our troop we would be the only tank to find our way down the escarpment to take the strip. Apart from the plane landing, there was not much activity to be seen. The sandstorm created a cover for us as we found our way down. When we got onto the runway about six Italians came out with a white flag. They stood a fair way from our tank. Yorkee ordered me to go out to them and make sure they were not armed. I drew my revolver and got down in front of our

71

tank. I beckoned to them to come over, but they would not move. I started to walk over to them when a machine gun opened fire to the right of me. Dusty opened fire from the tank onto the Italians. By this time I would have broken all records getting back to the tank. Yorkee called for the other tanks which soon came down and we took the strip, but unfortunately with no prisoners. The infantry took over and we continued on to Derna.

The Italian aircraft were Fiat CR42s and our aircraft were Gladiators. There was hardly a day passed by when we saw some very dramatic dogfights. It was during one of these that a CR42 was hit and trailing black smoke. He was losing height and the pilot must have decided to go out over the sea and ditch the plane. After going out a fair way he appeared to start to gain a little height. He changed his mind and turned to come back over land, very slowly still gaining height. He was hoping to clear the top of the escarpment on which we were sitting. As he approached, Dusty opened fire with the machine gun. The pilot did not gain enough height to clear the top even by a few feet, and crashed. Dusty claimed he was responsible for bringing him down. I thought the poor devil could not just get that extra few feet. It is hard to imagine what would have been passing through that pilot's mind.

The Italian planes now came over in force, and our aircraft were bringing many down. We heard that Derna had been evacuated so we were ordered to turn south back into the desert. We were having clutch trouble again with Bolton III, as we did with Bolton II, so Bill again filled one fire extinguisher with petrol and injected the clutch when required. We were travelling along one day when there was an explosion under the tank and a track came off. When we got out we saw quite a number of what appeared to be thermos flasks lying around. By the tank, we found some pieces which had once been one of these flasks, and we knew then they were mine-bombs dropped by an Italian plane away in front of us.

We got the track back on, but before we could move three planes started to drop more bombs and machine-gun us. The turret was being traversed for Dusty to return the fire with our machine gun. Dusty shouted to Yorkee that the back of our tank was on fire. Seeing the smoke, the planes left us as we jumped out and Yorkee grabbed the extinguisher. Although we had several, he had grabbed Bill's with the petrol in it. He sprayed a little on the fire and realised what had happened when the flames went higher! They had set fire to our bedrolls in the rack. However, we managed to get the fire out and Yorkee was OK.

Now we had to clear a way through the thermos flask bombs. Some were quite near, and these Dusty blew up with the machine gun while we were all inside the tank for protection. Yorkee then had a field day with his rifle. In fact he let us all have a few shots. It was the first time I had fired an army rifle, but with it we cleared a path to carry on.

It was during this move down into the desert that we came across some very nice fountain pens lying in the sand. We had already heard about these, as several chaps had lost a hand picking one up. The Italians left many booby traps during their retreat. Oases and any water wells had also been poisoned. It was very cold. Some of the wireless operators had found a way to alter the wireless sets to receive the BBC Home Service. This, of course, was not legal. Only headquarters heard any news from home. It only took a few minutes to alter the set. Yorkee was outside doing his two-hour guard and we were inside with our earphones on, listening to a programme broadcast from the Blackpool Tower. In between items messages were being given out to forces overseas. We heard the message that Trooper Bill Meadows' wife had given birth to a boy. We shook hands and congratulated Bill. When Yorkee's shift finished, he asked if there was any news. We had a feeling he knew what we had been up to, but turned a deaf ear. The next morning headquarters sent a chap over in a truck to tell Bill the news – we were so surprised!

One day a truck came round to our tank with mail. Yorkee got a letter and went and sat on his own to read it. All of a sudden we heard him shout 'The rotten bastards.' His wife had written him a letter also enclosing a threatening letter from a furnishing company, saying that they would take him to court unless overdue monthly payments were settled by return of post. It was very funny to see him waving this letter, sitting on an empty petrol can in the middle of the Western Desert. Yorkee was learning to play a mouth organ. It was well known by the rest of the squadron. One afternoon, everyone had to attend a lecture by Major Carlton. Our squadron of tanks were to move early the next morning before daylight to a position outside a large collection of Italians and Libyan troops with tank support they had been gathering together at this point for a few days. The idea was that we should get as close without them knowing we were in position a few miles from their camp. No noise was to be made, and Major Carlton remarked, 'I don't want to hear any bloody mouth organs playing.'

It was strange to hear the noise of the tanks the next morning and then suddenly all was quiet. There was no reaction from the camp. There were many other units all in place. We got the order just as daylight was breaking to start engines and advance. The whole operation was a complete surprise. We were inside the camp firing at their tanks, which had not even got started. Yorkee was firing away with his rifle from the top of our tank. Some got away, but the main lot were killed or captured, with the same old headache – what to do with thousands of prisoners.

It was soon after this action that our tank was ordered to go south on our own. We would be gone for two or three days to gather information. I was given an extended aerial as we were way over 13 miles and I would be sending messages back by Morse. In fact, some messages I sent back were 70 miles from base. We carried extra petrol in four-gallon cans and extra water, tea bags and of course bully. We encountered three Italian tanks on our second day out as we came over a sand dune; they were down in a dip. It looked as if they had stopped for a brew-up, so we went down and circled round them. Dusty was firing away, but as the Italian tanks tried to line their guns on us they each in turn lost a track. They were still firing with their machine guns, but soon all were killed. I got a pistol off an officer. Many of the Italian tank crews carried small tins of jam. It made a nice change on our biscuits. Soon after we had moved on, we saw what we thought was a mobile home being towed

74

by an Italian lorry with some Italians on board. We fired on the lorry, killing some of the Italians, and the rest surrendered. When we opened the door to the home we had a surprise to find seven women in a state of shock. It turned out that they were prostitutes employed by the Italian Government. They were being moved from one camp to another. We disarmed the Italians and, as Yorkee spoke a little Italian, we pointed which way to go and sent them on their way. This was all we could do. We reported back to base.

On our way back to base one of our planes came very low over our tank and dropped a message – 'Eyes report large columns moving from Benghazi on the coast road to Tripoli'. Yorkee gave me a message to send back to headquarters informing them of this news. When we arrived back B echelon were replenishing all the tanks. We had orders that we would all be moving that evening, going south and travelling overnight to arrive at a given point on the Tripoli road, south of Benghazi by dawn. No help was to be given to anyone breaking down. Once we had started, we were joined by more and more units. We now knew the Italians were pulling out from Benghazi with all they had left. We arrived at a point off the road before dawn, and we found a position where we could not be seen from the road. Across the other side of the road was the sea. The place at which we had arrived was called Beda-Fomm. As it started to get light we were looking up towards Benghazi and could see a cloud of dust on the horizon rising up into the sky.

The road opposite to where we were sitting was built up across a very large dip about half a mile long. It was built up in places to about ten feet. It was arranged that the road would be blown up on the Tripoli side when the columns were in the dip. Very soon we saw the enemy columns coming towards us along the high part of the road. On each side of the columns were bunches of Italian tanks very close together. Also on the road were large artillery guns and lorries. We were looking at what was left of the Italian army in Libya. The whole column must have stretched for several miles along the road. As the road was blown up we came out of our positions and took on their tanks. This was the first and what proved to be the last time that their tanks had traversing turrets with a fairly large gun. On the road there was complete panic as they tried to turn the guns and vehicles around, and a lot toppled off the road. Many of their tanks were being knocked out.

The battle of Beda-Fomm lasted all that day. A lot on the other side of the road were driven into the sea. There were large pockets holding out and some tanks still operating. It was starting to get dark when we came face to face with an Italian tank and quite a lot of infantry following it. The tank must have seen us first, as he fired and hit the front of our turret. The shell did not come in but left a gaping hole in the front. We had to evacuate the tank, and the infantry took us prisoners.

They took us to a spot away from the battle and left two Italians to guard us. We lay down and, because we were so tired, we went to sleep. When we woke, we were on our own. The two guards had gone. There was still some gunfire, but we made our way back to our tank and got all our personal things off. The road where the action had taken place was a terrible sight. All around us there were so many dead and no end of tanks with the crews dead inside. As there was very few infantry supporting us we were given the job of burying the dead, or what was left of them. It was not easy getting them out of the tanks. There was a chap in our squadron who always spoke and acted as if he had no fear of anything. In some of the burnt-out Italian tanks were bodies half-burnt. Sometimes we would tie a rope around what was left and pull the half body out of the tank. This chap was with us helping with recovery and burying these bodies. At one stage we pulled part of a body out and the legs had been burnt. One of these fell off, and he picked it up with both hands and held the leg up to his mouth as if he was eating it. It so happened that as he opened his mouth, he misjudged what he was doing and it did go into his mouth. We all shouted to him to stop, as it was a disgrace to our squadron the way he was carrying on. However, it must have played on his mind, for within a week he was on his way home in a straitjacket – completely mad! We stayed there for a week doing this gruesome task.

Burying the dead was not an easy task as, near the coast, it becomes very rocky, and we were lucky to dig down in the sand about two feet. We then laid the corpse in and covered it with sand, and collected and built rocks over the graves, otherwise the desert rats and other wild animals found in the desert would soon find the corpse. All around us were large Italian lorries with open tops, all kinds of vehicles, tanks, motorcycles, littered everywhere as far as the eye could see. I got on an Italian motorcycle with two panniers on the back. As we were using up all the rocks in our area, I could go out to collect rocks in the panniers. It was while I was out on my own that I was shot at by a bunch of Italians holding out. I returned, and a tank went out to round them up. While we were burying the dead, a truck came to a stop. In it was a driver and a captain who we did not know, from another unit. As the captain had come along towards us he had seen some Libyan looters on the back of some lorries. As he shouted to us, a Libyan stood up in an open lorry near us. The captain ordered me to shoot him, as I was the nearest, and he ordered Bill and Dusty to shoot some others quite near. Now I am sure I had been responsible for killing perhaps hundreds in our actions, but being loader of both guns in our tank, I did not see those being killed. Yorkee would pop away with his rifle and Bill, the driver, could see. I could not chicken out, so I drew my revolver. When the Libyan saw me, he was getting over the side of the lorry, and I fired three rounds and he fell down dead. When the other looters heard my shots, they fled. We saluted the captain, and off he went. Dusty said, 'Bloody hell! That's another one we have to bury!' We never saw any more looters in our area.

It was during this week that I managed to get four Italian Baretta pistols which were used by Italian officers. It was later, during an action with the Germans, that I got hold of a German Luger. I stripped all of these and wrapped all the parts in oily rags and kept them by the side of my wireless set under my stock of cigarettes. I was hoping that they would go into a museum on one of our ships.

The Germans had now landed in Tripoli and large columns were on their way from Tripoli to Benghazi, which was approximately 1,000 miles. With the heat and the flies in the day we were pleased to see the end of that week. Our tank was not fit for repairs, so we set it on fire and left it there.

Most of the tanks that had taken part in the action had now come to the end of their operational lives. Most were requiring spares, but only a few went back on transporters. This became a slow process. We were travelling on lorries or any other transport that was going back. The Germans were catching up very quickly, and it soon became clear that it was we who were now retreating. Although advancing over 500 miles during the whole of Wavell's campaign, we had never received any spares. All the tanks had simply run themselves into the sand, and many stayed there and may still be there today!

It was a sad end to a brilliant campaign led by a brilliant General who had not received any back-up. On the retreat we mainly kept to the coast road. German planes were over every day. Apart from that, we kept our noses in front. We stopped at Tobruk for an evening and night's rest. We were resting in rocks on the sea front when ships from the Italian navy opened up with a naval bombardment on us. This was one of the most terrifying experiences of my whole service. I was trying to claw into the rocks with my fingernails like so many others. In fact there were quite heavy casualties. The Australians held on to Tobruk and the Germans went on this time to El Alamein, where they halted, like us, out of spares and back-up. We went back to El Amiriya and were given a short leave in Alex. Just time to get cleaned up, beards shaved off and the blackheads on our faces and arms removed by electrical treatment. After the leave the squadron was made up to full strength, and at long last we received a new Cruiser tank which became Bolton IV.

It was early in June 1941 that we made our way back to the desert. As the Germans now held El Alamein, which meant a great section of the railway was also in their hands, we could only take the tanks a short distance by rail. Tobruk had now been surrounded for about three months with the Germans ringed round the outside and another ring of Italians, who had come up from Tripoli with them and were formed about a mile out from the Germans.

Wavell was still commanding the British forces and Rommel

the Germans. An offensive was planned for Sunday, 15 June 1941. The plan, as we were given to understand, was that Matilda heavy tanks were to take Halfaya pass and then to form the first wave in front of our Cruisers to break through the Italian and German defences to Tobruk, with the hope of relieving the Australians. We were to follow in to make the gap wider. We had taken Fort Capuzzo that morning and were now lined up waiting for the Matildas to arrive. A message was received that most of the Matildas had been put out of action at the pass, so at 12 noon we were still given the advance signal. As it was fairly flat ground we were able to get up a fair speed. We went through the Italian defences with very little bother. They still had no heart to fight and were glad to stand with their hands up as we passed by. We got into the German defences, and several tanks on each side of us were put out of action and were burning. Yorkee gave the order to Bill to pull over by the side of one that was burning, as his friend Captain Williamson was lying half over the side of his cupola with flames coming out of it. Bill stopped by the side, and Yorkee and myself jumped from our tank on to the back of the Captain's tank and lifted him on to ours. It was against orders to stop. We got back into our tank and began to move off and continued firing at the German guns. Then there was a tremendous explosion inside our tank. Whether the top was blown off our turret I'll never know, but I went straight out through the top and all I remember next was coming round on the ground by the tank with my face covered in blood. There was so much gunfire around me. I realised that I had been wounded in my head, back and foot. I had to get somewhere for protection. I did not see Captain Williamson again. When we lifted him over onto our tank his legs were almost burnt off. He was, I am sure, near to death then. As the shell went in the turret at the front and out of the back and he was lying on the back, one can only assume the worst.

About five yards from me was a burning tank. Crouched down by the side was a young chap who I knew was in our squadron, but I did not know his name. He was kneeling with his forearms on the ground. I shouted that I would crawl across

79

on the ground to him, but then his head just vanished. A shell must have taken it off. As I learnt later, German 88mm guns were sunk into the sand and rock with their nozzles just above ground level. Through stopping we had become a sitting duck.

I turned my head away and was wiping the blood out of my eyes so I could see more clearly when I saw Yorkee standing more or less over me, firing his revolver. One of his hands had been blown off. I turned my head to see what he was firing at. It was two Germans in a slit trench about ten yards away. As I saw them, one stood up with a small machine gun and opened fire. I saw Yorkee go down and felt a burning in my leg and knew I had also been shot again. As I looked out, there was another wave of tanks coming in. This wave of tanks never came fully into the German defences but inflicted heavy shell and machine-gun fire onto the Germans. They then turned around and withdrew and then another wave would carry out the same procedure. During this time I was lying in the middle of very heavy cross-fire. I tried to crawl to get by the side of a tank when the two Germans, now realising I was badly wounded, came and dragged me into their slit trench. It was a very shallow trench, and they were kneeling on me, firing their machine guns. I cannot remember how long the battle went on, but it seemed to die down and then start up again. There must have been more tanks coming in. It was during one of the quiet periods that the Germans spoke to me. They told me there would be an ambulance to pick up the wounded. I was surprised how well they spoke English.

Major Carlton had given the squadron a lecture on do's and don'ts when in action. He remarked that he had noticed in previous actions that when a tank was hit another tank would pull over to the side of it to give any help it could. This practice was to stop, as a tank is not an ambulance. Also you were putting another tank in a position where the enemy would have range to knock you out. We had put ourselves into a position exactly as Major Carlton had given orders not to, and we had paid the penalty for doing so. Yorkee's decision on that day, which we could not disobey, changed the rest of our lives and cost him his own.

Council school, Haywards Heath

J.W. Dinnage: Left to right, Jimmy, Author, Les, right: Petrol pump.

Allen Cobbins Air Circus, Hassocks 1929. My first flight.

International Stores, compulsory apprenticeship, 3 years 1930-33.

Black driving overalls,
Bovington 1939.

First leave home from Bovington
with Mother 1939.

On leave outside Star Hotel, Haywards Heath

Mother and Father, 1939.

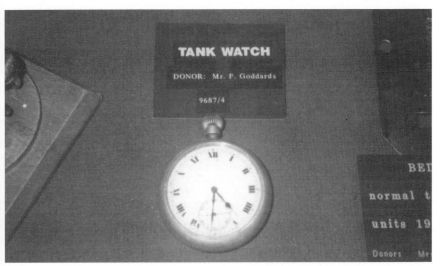

Tank watch removed before destroying our tank at Dunkirk

Doris age 19

No. CRRW/406/G
(If replying, please quote above No.)

Army Form B. 104—83A.

REPLY TO THIS CORRESPONDENCE
MUST BE ADDRESSED TO THE
O.C. CAVALRY & R.A.C. RECORDS.
AND NOT TO ANY INDIVIDUAL.

Cavalry & Royal Armd.
RECORD Record Office,
20 AUG 1941
OFFICE Station.
BARNET, HERTS. 19

SIR OR ~~MADAM~~,

I have to inform you that a report has been received from the War Office to the effect that (No.) _7889792_
(Rank) _Tpr._ (Name) _GODDARD Frederick_
(Regiment) _2nd Bn Royal Tank Regiment_
is a Prisoner of War _in the Middle East_

Should any other information be received concerning him, such information will be at once communicated to you.

Instructions as to the method of communicating with Prisoners of War can be obtained at any Post Office.

P. F. Goddard, Esq,
Woodlands
Victoria Rd
Hayward's Heath,
Sussex

I am,
SIR OR ~~MADAM~~,
Your obedient Servant,

RECEIVED
27 AUG 1941

F. W. Marriette
for Officer in charge of Records. Captain

IMPORTANT.—Any change of your address should be immediately notified to this Office. It should also be notified, if you receive information from the soldier above, that his address has been changed.

WL30241/1250 500M. 9/39. KJL/8818 Gp.698/3 Forms/B.104—83A/6

From records dated 20 August 1941, now P.O.W.

No. CPRW/511/G
(If replying, please quote above No.)

Army Form B. 104—83A.

REPLY TO THIS CORRESPONDENCE
MUST BE ADDRESSED TO THE
O.C. CAVALRY & R.A.C. RECORDS
AND NOT TO ANY INDIVIDUAL.

Record Office,
27 OCT 1941
OFFICE Station.
HICKEY, HERTS 19

SIR ~~OR MADAM~~,

I have to inform you that a report has been received from the War Office to the effect that (No.) 7889792
(Rank) Tpr. (Name) GODDARD, Frederick,
(Regiment) 2nd Bn. Royal Tank Regiment.
is a Prisoner of War now know to be wounded.
Nature of Wounds. Gun Shot Wounds Left Leg.

Should any other information be received concerning him, such information will be at once communicated to you.

Instructions as to the method of communicating with Prisoners of War can be obtained at any Post Office.

P.F. Goddard, Esq.,
"Woodlands"
Victoria Road,
Hayward's Heath
Sussex.

I am,
SIR ~~OR MADAM~~.
Your obedient Servant.

Marriette
for. Major
Officer in charge of Records.

IMPORTANT.—Any change of your address should be immediately notified to this Office. It should also be notified, if you receive information from the soldier above, that his address has been changed.

WL30241/1250 500M. 9/39. KJL/8818 Gp.698/3 Forms/B.104—83A/6

From records dated 27 October 1941, now wounded.

Wedding photo June 8th 1946. Left to right: Author, Doris, Squib, Aunt Gert.

Mr. Jenner, our neighbour at Victoria Road

Our family. Left to right: Dennis, Author, Valerie, Doris, Richard, Raymond.

My introduction to the Winters family, Ireland

Michael and Bridget Winters, Ireland.

Learning to fly, Biggin Hill.

Bill Quinn

Bill Quinn and Mike O'Hanlon

Author on opposite side of boat from shark.

Left to right: Pat Robinson Skipper, Michael holding shark.

Take-over of Ede's plumbing firm. Left to right: Lawrence, Michael, Richard, Ron, Raymond, Author.

Richard and Paddy, Council seats, Labour.

Doris and Author,
New Orleans.

Fred with Piper Warrior, Shoreham.

Private flying club, Londonderry, N. Ireland. Left to right: Noel, Author, Richard (Pilot), Michael, Frank.

Golden Wedding. Back row left to right: Dennis, Richard, Raymond, Valerie. Front row: Doris, Author

Bubbles

Balloon flight 31st July 1998. Back left: Richard, back 2nd left: Author.

Author by side of cruiser A13, Bovington.

Dennis and Family. Back row left to right: Phillip, Richard, Kristian. Front: Sylvia, Dennis.

Left to right: Mrs Flora Snowling, Doris, Anna Church (weight watcher instructor), Mr Christopher Snowling photo chairman Mid Sussex District Council. Doris at the presentation once she had achieved her goal in a sponsored slim to raise money for the British Heart Foundation.

The Winters family, back row left to right: Noel, Bridey, Brian, Michael. Front row left to right: Kevin, Nellie, Mrs Winters, Bernadette, Frank.

Valerie and Gordon's wedding
May 2nd 1981

Mike O'Hanlon and Margaret in garden at Ballindrait, Co. Donegal.

Raymond and Heather's
wedding March 21st 1998

Michael owner of 'The Mill House' restaurant Strabane, N.Ireland, my favourite restaurant.

Robert arriving home from
hospital for the first time.
Gillian, Robert and Richard.

SUSSEX GLIDING

This is to Certify that

Fred Goddard

has completed 1 instructional
flight(s) in a glider and is
considered suitable for further
training.

Instructor's signature

Roger Warn.

18/4/99

In fact it was not long after they told me this, that an ambulance arrived. There was still a terrible lot of gunfire, and as the ambulance arrived the firing seemed to get worse. There was a German medical officer going round and sorting out the wounded from the dead. I was picked up and thrown into the back of the ambulance. There was no equipment inside, and we were pitched on to the floor on top of each other. The officer gave the ambulance driver the signal to go. With that a shell came through the top of the ambulance and the ambulance driver was killed. The officer then got an open truck with a driver. We were pulled out of the wrecked ambulance and loaded on to the truck. We started to pull away when the driver of the truck was shot dead. The officer pulled him out of the seat and drove the truck himself into Bardia, where we were taken out and laid in a courtyard in a building where two German medical officers and their staff were operating.

It was not long before Bill and Dusty came in; both were walking wounded and came and laid down where I was. Dusty told me it was a shell which came in by the side of the wireless set and out the other side. He had just turned round and the shell had gone across his chest. The scar was still there when, by chance, I met him years later. Bill had a shrapnel wound in his arm. There must have been several hundred different nationalities wounded in the yard. The two officers came out from time to time with their orderlies, and would only have the ones taken in who needed immediate amputation, irrespective of their nationality. There was a terrible lot of screaming coming from inside the building and in the courtyard. I was in a lot of pain, more so from my left foot. I still had my army boots on, so I asked Bill if he could take my left boot off. He took a look at my boot and said, 'It's your own bloody fault for joining the army.' We lay in the courtyard until the next morning, when eventually they picked me up and carried me in on a stretcher. It was a great relief when they cut my boot off. The back of the boot and my heel had been blown off and the foot had been swelling up. There was a piece of shrapnel stuck in my skull, but they ignored that. They thought my left leg was broken and took me into another room, where they plastered my leg from

81

the thigh down to the ankle. They left a window in the plaster where they thought the bullet had gone in. They were not concerned about the shrapnel in my back. When they had finished with me, another one was brought in. I was given coffee and laid back out in the courtyard.

7

POW North Africa

Later that day we left Bardia for Derna. We stopped overnight
at a small building, where we had to lie on the floor. There were
two English officers and about ten other ranks. One of the officers protested to a German officer that I, as a wounded POW.
should be given something to lie on. There were some German
soldiers in another building who were sleeping on wooden
bunks. It was arranged that I could sleep on one of the bunks.
Our officer carried me over his back to the bunk bed. There
were about 20 German soldiers in the room, but one was a
Hitler Youth. As soon as he saw me he came over and would
have cut my throat if it had not been for two of the German
soldiers, who got him away. One of the Germans spoke some
English and assured me he would not be allowed near me. I
gathered they could not get on with the Hitler Youth. I never
slept that night!

We moved on the next morning, travelling in a covered lorry
lying on the floor. My leg was becoming more painful under the
plaster. An Australian medical officer who was on the same
lorry, told me that at the next stop he would ask about getting
the plaster off. This he did. The Germans told him they had no
medical tools to do this. He explained that if they would let him
have a small knife of any kind, he would take it off. They agreed
to this and gave him a penknife, and he very soon had the plaster off. The leg was very swollen, and he said the bullet would
have to come out or gangrene would set in and the leg would
have to come off. He explained the bullet was not very far from

83

the surface and it would be very painful for a short time. He managed to sterilise the knife in a flame from a German's lighter. Several chaps held me down. Eventually I must have passed out with the pain, but when I came round he gave me the bullet. We had no dressings, but I held some cloth over the wound. We soon arrived in Derna, where they dressed my wounds.

It was here the Germans apologised for having to hand us over to the Italians. It became very obvious that there was no love lost between the Germans and Italians, in fact the Italians carried out all the donkey work. Before we were handed over, the Germans interrogated each one of us. I was carried into a room on a stretcher, and they asked me for my name and regiment and when we had left England. I told them I only need to give my name and army number and rank. After a while several German officers were talking together in German, then one officer told me I was a trooper with the Second Battalion RTR, also when we went to France, when we arrived home from France and when we had left Liverpool. In fact everything he said was true, but I did not react to any of it. Anyway they shook my hand, wished me luck – of which, up to now, I had received more than my fair share.

The Italians informed us they were waiting for more POWs to come in, and all together there would be 300 of us to be transported to a camp south of Tripoli. From this camp we would be taken over to Italy.

Now that the plaster was off and the leg was not broken, I was able to walk with the aid of two sticks which somehow one of our men got hold of for me. We were loaded into Italian covered lorries and set off, three lorries leaving at different intervals. The whole journey was expected to take about one week.

The heat and flies were playing havoc with the wounded. On each lorry were two guards who sat at the rear, and another who sat with the driver. There was talk of overpowering the guards and taking over the three lorries, but this idea was not on owing to the spacing of the convoy and the number of wounded. Each day at around noon we stopped, the mobile kitchen was set up and we were given our one meal of the day – boiled macaroni

– this was to become our favourite meal for a long time to come. Although the convoy stopped for breakfast and evening meals, this was the only meal we were given.

Because of the pain from my wounds, I only ate a little, and then was sick, like so many other wounded. Several times a day we would have to get off the road to allow German convoys to pass. These would have landed in Tripoli and were on their way to the front line. We arrived outside Benghazi and the convoy rested while the wounded were taken a few at a time into hospital to have their wounds dressed. Although the Italians had very little in medical supplies, I asked through an interpreter if they would remove the shrapnel from my back and head. They answered that they did not have the equipment to do this. This hospital in Benghazi had been bombed to the extent that there was very little left of it. They did do all they could and told us we would receive more treatment when we arrived in Tripoli.

We still had a long way to go. The guards were getting bored and were inclined to take it out on the POWs by butting them with their rifles for very little reason. We had now lost several wounded, who had died from their wounds. These were buried by the side of the coast road, and records were kept by our senior officer. Rumour, from one lorry to the other, was that we would be going to a camp about 60 miles below Tripoli down in the desert. The heat was almost unbearable during the day and the flies even worse.

It was while I was turning my dressing on my leg wound, this was the only thing we could do, to keep turning the same dressing, hoping to find a clean spot to put over the wound, that I noticed what were to become my best friends, maggots, in the wound. The Australian officer who had taken the bullets out was on our lorry, and I asked him what I could do about them. He told me they were the best thing I could have, as they would eat all the rotten flesh away and keep the wound clean. I had a lot of faith in what he told me. He had done a lot of good work for the wounded and was given permission to change lorries to help the wounded on the long journey. None of the other chaps wanted to sit by me because of the maggots. I put some of them on my back, because that was causing me trouble. If a wounded man had heard about my maggots and thought it a good idea, I would pass a few on to his wound. I would only let the fat ones go, I kept the lean and hungry ones.

We left the main coast road and headed south. After several hours we arrived at Tarhuna camp. We were put into three very large ground floor buildings with concrete floors. There were some other POWs already there, waiting to be shipped over to Italy, and they told us how the camp was run by a number of Italians with an Italian captain, who in turn worked under a German commandant, who also had his own staff. The captain loved to show off to the Germans how cruel he could be. We slept on the floors and had a very limited water supply. There was only water in a standpipe outside for a short time during the day. We would fill our dixies and do what we could with it, saving some for drinking. At 11 each morning everyone had to parade outside to get the macaroni lunch. No one could get a double helping, so if anyone was not in the parade they would not get their share. There were two coppers set up with fires underneath. Each copper was filled with water and macaroni, which was boiled up. By noon the temperature outside could rise to 110–120 degrees F, and many passed out on the parade and were helped by our own chaps, who were fitter. Some who passed out at the last moment were left lying. At 1 o'clock the Italian officer would arrive with his underdogs. Some tomato juice would be added to one copper only. The interpreter then instructed that there were to be two queues formed at each copper. All Roman Catholics to the copper on the right, with tomato juice, all others to the left. There were around 400 men lined up in the queues. The underdog would wipe a spoon with a clean cloth and hand it to the captain, who took a spoonful from each copper and made out he tasted it. In fact he threw it into the sand. A ladleful would be given to each man.

The first day they cut all our hair off. I still had the shrapnel in my skull, so they shaved the hair off round it. I was still managing to get around with the two sticks. Although the wound in my leg was beginning to heal, my leg was swelling up from the foot upwards. One chap who I was sitting talking to remarked about the pumping noise he could hear from my leg. This was

86

the first time I realised how deaf I was, although I had had a ringing in my ears since the explosion in the tank. This I learnt later was nerve deafness from the blast.

There was no medical help at this camp, and after a few days the senior officer of the POWs insisted on seeing the German commandant. It was then arranged that all the wounded would be taken into Tripoli to receive treatment and returned to the camp. We were loaded up into two lorries and driven the 60 miles into Tripoli under armed guard. We arrived at the hospital and were taken in two at a time. My turn came round and I was taken into a room and laid on a table. I was surprised that there did not appear to be anything in the room. Two chaps came in and looked at my wounds. I still had my maggots! They went back out and reappeared with two other chaps. They had me face-down on the table, and one had something like a large pair of pliers or tongs. He managed to get hold of the shrapnel which was embedded in my skull and pulled it out. They were all laughing and I was screaming with the pain, although it did not last very long. I soon recovered and made them understand about my back. They held me again, and eventually he removed more shrapnel. An interpreter explained to me later that they had no anaesthetic, but decided not to tell me before attempting to remove the shrapnel. It was a great relief to know both pieces were now out.

We then returned to Tarhuna. After a few days back, and owing to the terrible conditions we were living in, a lot of the men developed dysentery and died. We now had unwanted friends – lice. I still had my maggots but did not tell the others. The strange thing that I could not understand was that most of the chaps would not accept maggots but were happy picking out lice. I only wished the maggots would eat the lice!

One day we were taken out, one by one, to the German side of the camp. Here we came under a very strict interrogation as to whether we were in anyway Jewish or related to Jews and, as I also learnt later, they believed there were some sailors who were responsible for machine-gunning some Italian sailors who were in the water after their ship was sunk. In turn the English ship had been sunk and some of the survivors had been captured. This interrogation went on for several days. Each morning before daylight an Italian firing squad would come in where we were sleeping and take out several chaps whom, we assumed, were Jewish. They were given spades to dig their own graves, and all we would hear was the noise of the shots. The Italians who carried out these executions would come back singing. The senior POW officer and other officers under him were keeping records of the men who were taken from our building and shot, and of the names of those responsible. Some of the chaps who were friendly with the victims were able to give the officers details. Protests were made to the Italian captain who, one morning, gave out through his interpreter, that if we kept complaining, he would shoot the lot of us. I have always hoped he was brought to justice after the war had ended.

We stayed in Tarhuna for six weeks. All the wounded and a selection of others left for Tripoli, but we left many behind, hoping they would soon follow. We were put into the hold of a ship where there were wooden bunks three tiers high. It was very hot. There were rumours that the ship was one of Italy's luxury liners, the *Rex*, which had been converted to a troop ship. After six weeks in Tarhuna we were all in very poor shape. Everyone had lost a lot of weight. The hold on the ship was kept in darkness most of the time, and this became a glory hole for the lice with the heat. We kept our fingers crossed that we would get across to Italy without any of our own naval ships having a go at us. We gathered there were plenty operating in the Mediterranean. The Italian guards in the hold were very nervous the whole trip. I cannot remember how long the journey took across the Med to the south of Italy.

We docked at a port which we thought was Taranto. It was a great relief to get out of that hold and to find we had arrived in a normal climate. We had left behind the heat and the flies. Over the next few days we travelled in open lorries part of the way and the rest by train.

8

POW Italy

We arrived at a place called Capua, which we found out later was about 20 to 30 miles inland from Naples. Here we had to walk several miles to a new POW camp. This camp was situated at the foot of the volcano, Mount Vesuvius. I still had my two sticks, but after that walk my leg was swelling up really badly. There were a few POWs in the camp, and who should be there but Bill and Dusty. Bill's arm was not very good. Dusty's chest had healed up fine. I had not seen Bill or Dusty since Bardia. They had not been in Tarhuna but at another camp west of Tripoli on the coast road.

Altogether there were now 400 prisoners in Capua, with more coming in each day. This camp had not been registered with the Swiss Red Cross. Since we had been taken POW all the other camps were only transit camps. Capua was to be our first permanent camp, with double barbed wire fencing and machine gun outlooks. It was early in September 1941 when we settled into this new camp. There were some huts and tents with straw mattresses, and most of the wounded were put into huts while the fitter ones slept in the tents, which were only temporary while more huts were being built. In the huts we had wood-built bunks. Outside was a long trough with standpipes for washing. Behind the troughs were screens so one could have a washdown. Outside toilets were behind screens. These were just large holes in the ground which were dug out from time to time by POWs and loaded into sewage trucks which came in through the main double gates of the camp. About 50 yards outside the main gates was what looked like a steam train with a very high chimney. It was, as we were to find out, a steamer for de-licing.

Most of my wounds had now healed over, the only one that would not was on my heel. Now we were in Italy, I noticed my maggots had deserted me. They really had done a good job! If only the lice would do the same.

We received our helping of macaroni each day on the same lines as we used to at Tarhuna, two coppers, one with tomato juice. There was no doubt now that this was the ruling menu for POWs. We had to parade outside each day for roll call. The Italian commandant gave out the usual speeches – if anyone escaped and was recaptured what would be the penalty. This could be so many days staked out in the sun and then transfer to another camp. Mainly the camp would be run internally by our own senior officers, who in turn would be responsible to him. One of the first protests made by our officers was that the camp must be registered with the Red Cross.

There were four chaps who came from the Swiss Red Cross and took particulars of every prisoner in the camp and details of the wounded. They told us that from now on the Italians must attend to the wounded each day. There were a lot who needed hospital treatment urgently. Working parties were arranged for the fittest, who went out from the camp in groups of about 20 to 30 at a time to work in the fields for farmers. These chaps would get extra food from the Italian civilians, which some would bring back to share with others not so fortunate.

Vesuvius was very interesting to watch, particularly at night. It was still very warm in the day, but more of a comfortable heat than in North Africa.

It was not long before only one at a time of the badly wounded was taken from the camp to a hospital. If it was a case of amputation, this would be carried out, and when the chap had recovered enough he would be brought back on a stretcher with the limb wrapped in newspaper, which had to be buried somewhere in the camp. At first, an Italian medical officer would go round the camp attending to the wounded; then it was decided that all walking wounded would report sick at 10 o'clock each morning at a table in the open, where two Italian medical orderlies would treat us. One of the orderlies was an interpreter. I joined the queue each morning on my sticks, and like everyone else was given an aspirin. As far as the Red Cross were concerned, we had received treatment.

Soon we received our first Red Cross parcels. These were given out by the Italians, one parcel to each man. When we received this it really boosted our morale. In the parcels, as far as I can remember, were tea bags, dried milk, coffee, tins of jam, sugar, 50 Gold Flake cigarettes in a round tin, corned beef, a tin of soup and salt and pepper. These made a big difference to our lives, and in particular to two chaps who were always exchanging things from their parcels with others. We received these parcels about every two weeks, but sometimes it would be longer. The Italians were mad to get coffee from the parcels. They would exchange anything to get coffee.

Many of the chaps who, like myself, enjoyed a cigarette, were quite willing to swap some of the food for cigarettes. One of the chaps, who was an Australian medical orderly called Amos, and another English orderly called Peter, soon built up a stock and it become well known that they were trading with the Italian guards. This was against the orders laid down in the camp and was considered as a crime to be answered to if ever we returned to England. They had been in front of our own officers and warned about this practice. Amos and Peter did not work together, in fact they were in competition with each other. The other thing that was noticed was that they were not long in learning to speak Italian and were often seen talking to Italian officers.

There was an escape committee formed. It was against the rules for anyone to try an escape without putting their plan before the committee. If their plan was accepted, they would then be helped. The first two to go were sailors, but they were caught at a railway station in Rome. They had done very well as they must have travelled about 100 miles to get that far. They were brought back to Capua and staked out for two days. No one was allowed to go near them. Staked out meant they were laid out on the ground with arms and legs outstretched. Four

91

wooden stakes were driven into the ground and the wrist, and ankles would be tied to stakes. They would only have a pair of shorts, so there was no protection from the sun. At night it was very cold. After two days they were taken away to another camp. The idea of staking them in our camp was to deter any others from trying to make an escape.

Each week we had to parade in batches of about 30 at a time, naked but carrying any clothes that belonged to us in a bundle. Throughout the day each batch would be taken out of the camp to the steamer. Here we would be shaved head to foot. While we were being shaved our clothes would be in the steamer de-lousing. This worked very well if it was our batch that went early in the day when the old rocket, as we called it, had plenty of steam. Later in the day, afternoon and evening, it was hopeless, as there was not enough steam because the Italians had let the fire die down. So, instead of killing the lice, it hatched more and one came back worse off.

As I have said, Vesuvius was quite interesting to watch at night time but it soon became a nightmare for us. Naples was about 20 miles or so from Vesuvius. Our planes would come in and bomb Naples. They then flew inland and turned round at Vesuvius. This was their guiding light to fly back home. The Italians retaliated by turning off the water supplying the camp for two or three days if there were air strikes two or three nights running. We could go a week without water. We did fill any vessels we could get hold of as reserves in case this happened.

My leg was now becoming more swollen, in fact, I was realising that unless something was done I could not survive the swelling and pain. Each morning I went on sick parade but only received aspirin. One morning, I went down and when I got to the table the orderly put an aspirin on to the table in front of me. I got my stick and brought it down on the table. At the same time I swore at the interpreter. I knew that for what I was doing I could have been shot. Having given this a lot of thought for several days, I had decided that this action was my only hope for survival. I had seen three Italian medical officers standing talking inside the main gates, and I was trying to attract their attention. I continued shouting, and some of the other chaps on

92

the sick parade also joined in shouting. One of the officers came across and through the interpreter wanted to know what the trouble was. While the interpreter was trying to play everything down the officer was looking at my leg. This officer was a captain, and he told me he would come back later that day to see me in my hut. I thanked the chaps who had helped me gain this officer's attention. I did not expect he would come back, but he did later that day, and gave my leg a check over. He had brought an interpreter with him, who explained what the captain would like to do. He had already consulted a colonel since seeing me that morning. They would, with my consent, take me into an Italian hospital where they would, after a further test, carry out an experimental operation. In his opinion the artery had been damaged.

They would open the leg up to find where the damage was, and repair the artery with a silver clip. As the leg was so blown up the chances of this being successful were very small, and they would have to remove the leg if necessary. I had no alternative but to agree to whatever he wished. Really, I was thankful that something was going to be done. My action at the sick table that morning had achieved some results. I did see our own commanding officer in the camp to inform him as to what was happening. He wished me luck and told me he would be making inquiries as to my progress.

Our first batch of letters arrived in Capua. I received two letters, one was from our chaplain (or as we called him, Padre), who had received the news that I was a POW. Although he knew I really was not a religious man, we did have the occasional chat together when in the desert, mainly about my younger days. He, himself, was married with two small girls. It had taken about two weeks for his letter to find me. I appreciated him writing, it was a contact from the past. My other letter was from Dot, informing me she had met a Canadian and was going to be married and live in Canada – I was not impressed!

There were just a few more POWs arriving from time to time at our camp and it was a big surprise when, two days after receiving the letter from the Padre, he was brought in. He had

93

been out in his truck visiting some of the tank crews in our squadron which had been leagued out far apart. As the sun went down he went on to the next tank, but got lost. It had become very dark, and he saw what he thought was an English small column and followed it. It turned out he was behind a German column, and was captured. As there was not a padre in Capua, he was pleased to take the services. It was surprising how many chaps had changed their religion because of the tomato juice!

The queue at that copper got longer each week, and although it is surprising what a little extra flavour can do, we were still hungry. Amos and Peter were always first in the tomato queue. They had now become very disliked because of their fraternising with the Italians. Although they were being outcast by most of the men, there were quite a few others who continued to trade with them, they in turn traded with the Italians.

In early November 1941, I was taken from the camp, on my own, in a small truck with an armed guard. I believe it was about two hours from the camp to a large hospital at Caserta. On the journey I realised this was the first time for a long time that I was on my own. I soon realised I was missing something. I had not appreciated until now the comradeship of the other chaps around me, who were always so helpful. On arriving at the hospital I was put into a room on my own with a bed. I had not lain on a bed like this for what seemed years. The captain who was responsible for me being there came in with the colonel and an interpreter. They explained again what they hoped to do, and also that a nun would come to see me to take particulars and for me to sign a consent form for the operation, which would be carried out the next day. The captain told me he had cancelled his leave that week to be at the hospital for my operation. The nun came later that day to take my particulars. She spoke fairly good English, but when she asked me my religion and I said 'C of E', she pointed both her thumbs down to the floor. In other words I could go to hell. I said, 'Not today, but perhaps tomorrow!' I signed the consent form.

I had a good sleep in the bed that night, but woke up very early the next morning as there seemed to be so much activity around me. My leg was shaved from the hip down. I also had a shave and a very good wash. This was a real wash with hot water. I was put on a trolley and wheeled into the operating theatre. I remember as I was wheeled through the door, there was a clock which was at 9 o'clock. I was amazed when I was put on the table how many students were seated in a tiered half-circle, they could have numbered 50 to 100, to watch the operation. A medical chap and a female nurse introduced themselves in perfect English and explained that they were only there to talk to me or answer any questions I wished to ask. I said that as I would be asleep during the operation we would not be talking to each other much. They said I would be awake during the whole operation as I would be having a needle in my back which would paralyse me from the waist down, and assured me I would not feel any pain. The colonel and the captain were at the table, and I saw the colonel had this very large syringe in his hand. I was laid on my stomach and hoops were fixed over my shoulders, with my arms left over the hoops. I felt the needle go into my back and was soon paralysed. I had a long conversation with my interpreters. They had lived in England and learnt their nursing in London. They had now cut my leg open. I knew they had a tourniquet on, and they told me each time when they would release it. They told me the operation was going very well and they had found the artery and where it was damaged. The captain had a conversation with the interpreters, after which they asked me if I would like to see my leg open. I said I would, and some mirrors were brought in, and the two interpreters held the mirrors so I could see what was going on. The first thing I noticed was the amount of blood that seemed to be everywhere. The colonel was covered, and there was even some on the ceiling. The leg was open from above the ankle up to the knee, with rods across inside crosswise. This reminded me of a rabbit after it had been cleaned, hanging up in butcher's window with a stick across its stomach. There were three or four rods and the interpreter was explaining exactly what they were doing.

It was soon after this that I started to feel some pain. The paralysis was only to last for two and half hours and it was now 12 o'clock, so it was half an hour over time. The pain became

95

almost unbearable when they gave me a mask, which put me to sleep for a while. The operation was going well over its time. I think by then I must have had more Italian blood in me than English! Later they gave me another mask, and when I came round from this they told me they could not give me anything else as my heart would not take any more. Everything was now done except the stitching up. They now tied me down on the table and I was screaming with the pain. I asked for the leg to be taken off, but they kept asking me to hang on a little longer and it would soon be over. As I found out later, they had 14 inches to stitch and clip.

At last it was over, and I asked the time. It was 1 o'clock and I was put back in the small room. There was another bed in it in which an orderly slept. I laid in the room for two weeks, hardly sleeping, but in considerable pain. This room was always kept in semi-darkness, and I wondered if it helped with my recovery. The captain called in from time to time, in fact he became very friendly because of how well everything had gone so far.

It was in the third week that I started to feel back among the living again. I was making very good progress. I must have been kept alive by being fed on a drip. For the first time since the operation I started to feel hungry. I mentioned to the orderly that I would like something to eat. He said he would ask the captain when he came in next time. When the captain came in he asked me if I would like to be moved to a large ward where there were all Italian wounded. I agreed to this, and I was moved straight away. The captain then asked me what I would like to eat, he said I could have anything I wished. I asked for chicken, which they gave me with some vegetables. It was a very nice meal, but I could only eat a small amount.

The ward was very large, about 50 beds, taking up all available space so there were beds each side, top and bottom. All were Italian. When they had visitors I felt like an animal in the zoo. They all used to stand and glare at me, as I was the only POW there and perhaps the first one they had seen. It was not long before, when they came in to visit again, they would bring me in some food or sweets. The captain went on his leave, and when he returned he brought his wife in to see me. I was given a pair of wooden under-arm crutches. I was having the stitches and clips removed a few at a time. It had been stitched up with five clips and five stitches. They left some weep holes in the back of the leg and these were left open with gauze plugs to allow the leg to drain out. I soon learnt to use the crutches but was not allowed to put my left leg to the floor. It was explained that I would have to be fitted with an iron support before I could put any weight on it. However, it was beginning to look a normal size and the pumping noise had gone.

I was returned to Capua camp. It was good to get back where English was spoken, but at the same time I had been spoilt at Caserta. The only wound that would not heal up was the heel, but it did not cause me any bother. When I had the weep holes dressed they did the heel. For some unknown reason it refused to heal up.

We received a parcel from time to time, but they were not coming very regularly. The camp had become more organised while I had been away. Bridge had become a favourite card game. Cards, jigsaws and some books had arrived through the Red Cross. Letters were arriving, and I received one from my parents. Early 1942 came with some more welcome news. A repatriation board would be coming to Capua from Switzerland with the view of exchanging the badly wounded who still required further treatment – mainly limbless who needed false limbs and non-combatants, such as the medical corps and clergy. The Italian medical officers, along with one of our own, would compile a list of those who were considered eligible to go in front of this board. From then on we lived on rumours and hopes of being included on the list. As I was told that I would need irons fitted to my leg and also at that time was still receiving treatment, I was keeping my fingers crossed. We were seen several times by our own medical board, and at last a list was put up and a date when the board would be at the camp. My name was on the list. This was a good booster for many of us who were on the list. It was almost stopped by the Italian commandant who came into camp each day. One day he had his small dog with him. After the commandant's parade, the dog was missing. They found the fur and bones over in a corner of the camp; as I have said before, it is strange what hunger can do! The commandant had the water turned off for a week. He threatened to stop the Swiss board from coming into the camp. The macaroni was reduced each day for a week. The Italian captain came to see me and was pleased how the leg had now returned to its normal size.

It was about April or May that the board arrived at Capua. All the wounded were seen first. When my turn came, I went in on my crutches. They spent a while looking at paperwork and then asked me to put my leg to the floor and show them how far I could walk. I told them, if I tried to do that I would fall on the floor and, since the operation, I had been told not to try this until I had been fitted with an iron support. This was not the only board we had to go in front of. In fact, we had to go in front of three boards with different medical personnel each time. The list each time got shorter as quite a few were rejected. My name was kept on.

Bill and Dusty had not been on any list. The day came when those accepted were told to get ready to leave. After saying our goodbyes the captain came to say goodbye, and I was very surprised to see him crying. However, I thanked him for all he had done for myself and others. The padre, Amos and Peter also came, although assurances were made with those we left in Capua that Amos and Peter would never get home. When Amos and Peter were told this they only laughed. I suspect they felt nothing could happen to them as they were more on the Italian side than ours.

9

Journey to Freedom

We left Capua for Parma, in the north of Italy, by train. The train journey was uneventful and we spent one night on the train. At some of the stations we stopped and the Italians, when they knew we were POWs, passed some food and wine in, but there were some who tried to stop them. We arrived in Parma and the place we were put in was a large disused garage which had a courtyard in the middle of the four sides. The history was that it had been a prison as all the windows had iron bars. Some of the men were already there, and altogether there were about 200 of us, all for repatriation.

We were now not far from the Swiss border. This place, we were told, was only a transit point where we would be leaving for home. Little did we realise that we would be there another year!

We again lived on rumours that we would be leaving the next day, week or month. There was a single-storey building at the rear of the garage in which there were about 80 beds. I was put in one of these. On one side of me was an Australian named Charlie Wallace, and on the other side was a South African, Len Ross. Charlie had a very bad leg wound but was able to walk without crutches. Len was in the hold of a ship bringing him and other POWs from North Africa which had been torpedoed and sunk. Len had managed to get out and swam to the Italian shore. They had been torpedoed at night, and Len found himself suffering from frostbite. In fact he had lost most of his toes.

At the front of the main building, from the road, were two

large doors. Inside the doors was the large courtyard. On each side were rooms, and there was a corridor with rooms each side. A staircase led from the corridor to rooms on the first floor. It was in these rooms that our own officers were put. There were two nuns who came in each day. They served the macaroni and looked after the beds etc. They had a small room on the first floor, where they had a sewing machine and would carry out sewing for the POWs. Amos and Peter were put in separate rooms off the corridor. There were guards all around the building, and soon we discovered that this building stood on its own with roads all around it.

The weather was very warm when we arrived, but in about November 1942 we had snow about two feet deep. We all thought by now that repatriation had been cancelled as there was no more news about it. Other POWs arrived, and some of these were not eligible for repatriation. At least they could give us up-to-date news on how the war was progressing. The Italians gave out news bulletins every week as to how they were winning the war. When they had won the war, we would be taken back to North Africa and put to work road-building. Most times during these news bulletins and lectures everyone would start singing, and they had to give up.

The nuns were concerned about my leg, as I was still losing a lot of blood from the weep holes. There were others who were not receiving any treatment on their wounds, and some were in a very poor way. Medical dressings etc. were very short and wounds were becoming very dirty, with old dressings being re-used and put back on wounds. Gangrene started to set in, and very soon some were dying through lack of proper treatment. The Italian medical officer could not have cared less. Those of us who were losing blood he gave each day a glass of vino. This was horrible to drink as it was very crude. There were not many that were allowed this.

At Parma, we kept up such things as Derby Day and Christmas Day, in fact any special days. Bridge again became very popular, and we now had a chessboard. The interpreter came in very excited one day. He had a parcel for myself, and when I opened it there were 200 Woodbines sent from the Wesleyan

Church in Perrymount Road, Haywards Heath, by Mr Langridge, the minister there. It was months since we had had any ciga- rettes. The interpreter offered me an exchange of three to one for the best of Italian cigarettes for the Woodbines (Italians were mad for English cigarettes). I agreed to this, but I kept some of the Woodbines and was very tempted not to have one, but I could not do that in front of the other chaps. It was like the United Nations in our room. We had Italians, Gurkhas, Australians, South Africans, New Zealanders and Canadians. It was certainly a mixed bag. The interpreter arrived back with 600 Stella cigarettes. These were shared out, giving everyone three each, Amos and Peter excluded, although no doubt they had cigarettes stored away. They very soon fraternised with the two nuns, who had quite a lot to say as to how things were run, and also with the Italian officers.

I had now become quite a good bridge player, and very soon one of our officers asked me to partner him in the bridge tourna- ments. This meant I was very often going up the stairs to the officers' quarters. Here we would play other officers so as to practice together. It was during one of these practice games that I was asked about the glass of vino I received each day. I said that sometimes I gave it to my friends Charlie and Len, it tast- ed so dry. Perhaps it was good for the blood, but I never drank enough to find out. They then took me into their confidence as to an escape that was being planned by four officers who felt capable of getting to Switzerland.

The small room the nuns used for needlework looked out onto the roof of the guard house. From this roof was a high wall that was built along by the roof of the guard house, and it was about three feet taller than the roof. This wall was built out to the side of the main gates. There would be a drop of about 12 feet off the end of the wall onto the road to the pavement out- side. The window had two or three iron bars. They had already obtained a pattern and had made a key to get into the nuns' room, and were now in the process of cutting the iron bars a lit- tle each night, camouflaging the cuts by filling with a made-up paste. The problem was getting the guards out of the guard room to give the men enough time to jump out of the window,

101

onto the roof and out onto the street. The timing had to be exact for the guards to be called out, leaving the main gate unguarded. The officers suggested that if I should save some of the wine, enough for about four of us to have a party, and cause enough noise for the guard to be called out. It was also to be at the furthest point away from the nuns' room and the main gate.

I told Charlie and Len only. We needed to get about four empty bottles, so we got on good terms with the dustmen who came in every other day. We explained the best we could, and they brought in six bottles. We started to save the vino. There were other chaps who did not mind giving us their ration. Every so often, we had spot searches, and they would come in any time of the day or night. Charlie and myself had the bottles in a cardboard box under our bed. When they came in to search, they always started searching our line of beds first, and Charlie's was before mine. As soon as they had finished with Charlie, I would push the box towards Charlie with my crutch and he would pull it under his bed with his walking stick. We had practised it so many times we never missed doing it exactly right.

I cannot remember the time the break was to happen, but I believe it was a few minutes past 10 at night. By then it was quite dark. Four of us got together at the furthest point we could at the end of our room. Very few knew what was going to happen, certainly not Amos and Peter. About an hour before, we started to drink the wine. Len did not drink very much, as his job was to watch the time and tell us. We became quite a nuisance to everyone around us. Who appeared but Amos and Peter, to try and quieten us down. Thing got very bad, and I remember having a go at Amos with my crutch. The guards were called out and we were taken back to our beds, only to learn the next morning that this time they left one of the guards in the guard house, and as the roof was corrugated iron he heard them drop on and raised the alarm. The four officers were caught out on the road and were sent away to another camp. I feel that if the Italians had not left one in the guard room, the officers would have got away. For our part, I thought we had done a good job.

The wine was stopped after this event, but no one was sorry

102

about that. For days after, if I drank a drop of water I felt bad again. Our lips were red for days.

Repatriation now became a thing of the past. No one talked about it any more, and quite a number of fit POWs were coming in. I decided that I would start learning to walk on my leg again, so at night I started by putting it onto the floor, and after a few weeks or so I could stand on it. After several weeks I was able to get around my bed. The weep holes had now almost healed up. I never put it to the floor during the day. It was early in 1943 that a notice was put up that the repatriation board would be sitting at Parma in the near future. My name was again included in the list. We did not get too excited about this. I suppose it became a matter of form and not a reality. The snow melted, and very soon we had very warm weather again. This was something that surprised us, the snow came around the same time each year and never melted until around a certain time in the spring.

The repatriation board came, and so many of us went in front of them again. We now treated it as a complete farce. Permission was given us to hold a concert party. Several got together to put on the concert, and I was asked to sing. An officer was having an upright piano brought in from outside for one day only, so the concert was arranged for the same evening. The piano was brought in and those who were involved spent most of the day in the concert room practising. The officer was the only one who could play a piano, and it seemed he only practised one tune – 'A Nightingale Sang in Berkeley Square'. The piano had not been tuned for years, but he worked very hard that day. I was to sing 'Blue Heaven'. I had never been involved in anything like this before, but it all seemed to be working out very well. About an hour before the concert was due to start, the interpreter came in with some of the guards and took the piano back out. He said that information had been given by some of our own chaps that an escape was planned for that evening. We never found out if it was Amos or Peter, but everyone sure it was one of them. This was done to put whoever it was further into the Italians' confidence. Anyway, after a lot of discussion between our officers and the Italians, the concert was allowed to take place without the piano. It was a success under the circumstances.

We had another two repatriation boards very close to each other, and our faith was restored once again that things were really on the move. It was early April 1943 that we were officially told who would be leaving. A list was read out of those who would be going, and my name was on the list. The Padre, who was also on the list, declined to go, as he said he would rather stay with those left behind. He had to be admired for making a decision to stay when he had a wife and two children. Amos and Peter were also on the list.

The morning that we left it was very early, and it was sad saying our goodbyes once again. I was still on crutches. Charlie and Len came up the passage with me. As we passed the door of Amos' room some Italians with a long box with four handles came out. We looked in the box, and it was Amos. He was dead. He had been poisoned, by the look on his face. There was quite a lot of spitting into the box. Peter was now becoming a very worried man.

Lorries were outside to transport us to the railway station. There were now exactly 199 prisoners. We were put on a train at Parma, and the rumour was we would be exchanged in Lisbon, Portugal. We had armed guards and arrangements had been made for sleeping on this train. When we stopped in stations, the Italians gave us food and wine. Not all the carriages were lucky, but everything was shared as fairly as possible. We went through a long tunnel under the Alps, and it was not long before we were in occupied France. At some of the stations the French also were passing food or drink onto the train. If there were Germans on the station they would stop the French from doing this. We noticed that very soon our train was if possible stopped in sidings rather than stations.

We travelled mainly along the south of France. We changed trains for the journey over the Pyrenees, having two engines to pull us. Once in Spain, when we stopped at a station or siding, we were not allowed to step off the train. If we had done, we would have been interned as Spain was a neutral country. There would be Spanish guards on each side of the carriages. We travelled through Spain and into Portugal, eventually arriving in Lisbon. We had now been a week on the train. By the side of our train there seemed to be hundreds of people. The surprising thing was that it was very early in the morning, about 6 or 7 o'clock, for so many people to be there. It seemed ages before we were allowed to get off. We waited by the side of the train for the Italian guards to get off, but they stayed on. People were shaking hands, and it was a dramatic moment for us when people were saying you are now free again, and for some time we could not move.

10

Back to Civilian Life

There were cups of tea and cigarettes in abundance. After a while things started to get organised, and we were put onto coaches and taken to hotels in Lisbon. I think it was about 50 men to about four hotels. I, like so many others, was surprised how many people spoke good English and how poor Portugal was. We were put into a large reception room, with tables set up with every kind of food one could have wished for, and coffee, tea and beer. Later that day, we would rejoin the coaches for a tour round Lisbon, then back to the hotel for an evening meal. After this we were to be exchanged in the main square in Lisbon and then taken to the hospital ship which would take us back to England. The problem with us was that we could eat only very little. Our stomachs could not take it. Some of the chaps were being very sick if they ate too much. We must have appeared a sorry lot after the work which had been put in to provide all the comforts. After a tour round Lisbon we were entertained back at the hotel and then taken to the square, where 800 Italians had been all day. Checks were made on numbers and we were exchanged, four Italians to each of us. The Italians were put on to the trains we had arrived on, and we were put on to the coaches and taken down to the docks. Here the hospital ship *Newfoundland* was waiting for us to board.

The ship had brought the Italians from England and had arrived that morning. It was a warm summer evening when we sailed out of Lisbon. They even had the band playing on the dockside as we left. We had very comfortable beds, which were welcome after a week on the train. We received new dressings on our wounds after having a good shave and bathing the best we could.

The next day was panic stations as someone was missing, and it did not take a second thought as to who! The strange thing about it was that all the records and medical history which had been compiled by the Italians, and was to have come home with us, had also vanished. Rumours were being passed around between those who knew Peter that, during that first night on board, all the records had been tied around Peter and he had been thrown overboard into the Bay of Biscay.

When it became known that the records had gone we knew the rumour was true, as now no one could be identified. I feel sure that no one in authority would miss Peter. No one would ever know he existed. It was only the ones who had come out of Parma who would know him or who could have helped Amos and Peter on their way.

The Red Cross provided comforts on the ship for the troops returning to England. I quote from the magazine *The Prisoner of War*, June 1943, '25,000 cigarettes, 10 dozen packs of cards, 600 treasure bags of toilet accessories, 600 1/2lb slabs of chocolate, 600 stationery sets with stamped envelopes and hundreds of copies of newspapers.' These were dated 7 and 8 June 1943, and the headlines were of the Eighth Army's breakthrough at Wadi Akarit, which was the prologue to the final drama of the North Africa triumph. We could not have been better looked after then by the Red Cross. It became very overwhelming at times.

After five days out from Lisbon, we arrived off the coast of England in the middle of the night. Early morning we arrived in Avonmouth. We were surprised that there was no one at the dockside, but it was not long before people began to appear. We had breakfast on the ship, and after that we were ready to disembark. It soon became clear that there was a hold-up as regards disembarking, and no one was allowed off the ship. The BBC was there, and by lunchtime the dockside was crowded and trains were drawn up on the dock sidings ready to take us to hospitals. It was early afternoon, and the first to disembark

107

were RAMC doctors and medical orderlies, then the stretcher cases were carried down, and then soon the walking wounded. As I stepped off the bottom of the gangway I was taken to one side to meet another soldier, who I was told would be my escort until I reached my home.

We went onto the train and a member of the Red Cross took all my particulars. It was then explained why there had been the hold-up before anyone could disembark. Owing to the loss of all our records, it had been necessary to bring in an escort for everybody returning from Italy. This chap, whose name was Jack, would be with me day and night until we arrived home and my parents signed a form to confirm that I was their son. He carried a warrant which, whenever we were travelling, would give us priority so that we would not be held up. I thought we would be going straight home that day, but this was not so. The date we had arrived back in England was 25 April 1943, and it was to be another three weeks before I would get home. I was with many others put on a train and taken to 104 General Hospital, Westbury, where Jack and I stayed for about a week. Jack and I got on very well together. I told Jack that when we got out of the station at Haywards Heath there was a pub across the road and we would have a drink in there before going to my home.

At the hospital they dressed my wounds and started to compile records. I was by now suffering with very bad bleeding piles, and with Jack I was taken to another hospital. I have always thought since that the long delay was checking on my past service, as apart from dressings, I had no further treatment. I was eventually given the all clear that I could go home on leave. I would be notified at home when and where I would have to report.

I was issued with a warrant. We got onto Victoria station, where I went to an Army Office to obtain some money. If it had not been for Jack, I do not think they would have given me any. He spoke up for me and, after several phone calls made by the Office, they gave me what I had asked for. I could not believe that after all I had been through here I was at home and pleading for money! All the time I was a prisoner I was being paid

108

my full army pay, and also I was supposed to receive one lira a day, which we have never received – not that it would be worth anything.

After having a drink together at Victoria station bar, we caught a train to Haywards Heath. When we came out of the station, my dream was completely shattered. Hanging on the door of the Burrell Arms was a notice, 'Sorry, Sold Out'. Things had altered so much while I had been away. It took some time to settle in.

We took a taxi and arrived at Woodlands. My parents had no idea I was coming, so it was quite a surprise for them. Jack decided to stay that night. My parents signed the forms, and we all went out to celebrate. The only pub open was the Star, so we spent the evening there. Jack went off the next day, and I spent the next few days visiting friends. It was not easy getting around with crutches, although I had become quite an expert on them. I spent about a month at home. I had not heard anything from the Army as to where I was to go. I realised that my wounds were not healing as they should do; the heel was causing me trouble, the piles were very painful, the weep holes on my leg were discharging again, and where they had started to heal up they had now opened again.

Hurstwood Hospital in Haywards Heath had been taken over by the Army, and in Holly Road quite near Woodlands was a sergeant who was in billets and was stationed at Hurstwood. I went up to see him one evening and asked if he could help me in any way. He came down the next day to tell me that they tried to find out about me, but no one knew I existed. He had, at the end of the day, managed to get me a medical appointment at Preston Park Barracks within the next few days. Meantime, he also arranged for me to go up to Hurstwood to have the wounds dressed. He also gave me a railway warrant to Brighton.

I went down to Brighton on my own, and I walked down from the station to the barracks on crutches. I thought back to the day when the colour sergeant had taken me from the barracks to the station in 1938. At the barracks I was shown into a room in which were about four medical chaps. An officer was seated at a table, and as soon as I heard him speak I knew that he was drunk. I then noticed glasses and gathered that they had all been drinking. At the end of the so-called medical examination, he announced that I would be classed as B3. I asked what did this mean exactly, and one of the chaps in the room answered, 'Fit for overseas service with light duties.' I could not believe my ears! I said that if caught again I would be shot, and they all laughed. I went home bewildered with the treatment I was receiving. I went to see the sergeant from Hurstwood again, and I let him read the letter I had been given about my medical examination. He also could not believe such a decision and said he would make arrangements to have me put in a military hospital within the next few days. It was not possible for me to go into Hurstwood, as this was a hospital which specialised only in head and brain operations, as it is today (1998).

About this time, Mr Randall, who was an engineer on the Electricity company, and who carried out a lot of good work for the British Red Cross, contacted me, as I was the first repatriated ex-POW to arrive back in Haywards Heath, and asked if I would make a speech at a rally being held by the Red Cross at Victoria Park to raise funds. The speech would give people an idea of what life was like in the camps and hospitals. One thing I have always avoided is public speaking, and more so at this particular time, as I was a nervous wreck. However, I felt that this was something I must do. I gave a fairly good description of conditions and particularly about the food parcels. The *Mid-Sussex Times* gave a full account of the speech, and Mr Randall was pleased with the results, so he asked if I would make another speech at the Perrymount Cinema, which I also agreed to do.

At last I felt things were improving when the sergeant came to tell me that he had a railway warrant for me to go to Epsom Hospital. This was a terrible hospital in the way it was run, the food was bad and I had to stay there for several weeks. I had two operations on the piles which only made them worse. The hospital was very dirty for a military-run place. I went home again to wait and see what would happen next. For the next few months I was at home, looking after the wounds as best I could.

The sergeant from Hurstwood had moved on, and although I went to Hurstwood to get help, they could not do a lot for me. At last I received a letter that I was to go back to Epsom to receive my discharge, and this I did and was discharged on 8 October 1943 – cause of discharge 'Ceasing to fulfil army physical requirements.'

I came home and went to see a doctor. I had registered with a Dr Dodd from Gander Hill who was responsible for me going into Roehampton Hospital, London, and at last I started to receive very good treatment. Some other chaps who were receiving treatment had also been in Epsom, and told me it had now been closed.

After several X-rays, it was discovered that I had quite a lot of pieces of shrapnel around my body. After most of this was removed, I started to walk on my legs without an iron and the weep holes healed up at last. The heel was still a problem, refusing to heal up. In between operations I was able to go home for a weekend. I received a War Disability Pension of 30 per cent, and this was paid from the date of my discharge. When I was in hospital this was increased to 100 per cent, but only for the time I was in hospital. I spent the next two years in and out of Roehampton. Once I spent a few weeks in the Star and Garter. While in this hospital I found that the chap in the next bed to me was from the First World War. He had lost both arms and legs. It was interesting to see how much he could do for himself. He had long sticks, and on the end of one he would have a razor and on the other a brush so he could shave himself and wash by lifting the sticks in his mouth, putting them between his leg stumps and controlling them with the move-ment of two short stumps. He had no family and told me he would be in that hospital, like so many others, for the rest of his life.

As my wounds had improved – the only one which was still open was my heel – I started to think about getting back to work. I went to the Electricity company and they agreed to give me a job on the switchboard at Electra House, Church Road, Haywards Heath. It was shift work, but at least it was a start. I could walk from Woodlands to Electra House with two walking sticks – that was about my limit. I was shown how to work the switchboard. I had not been there more than three weeks when I had to go back into Roehampton and have some more shrapnel removed from my back, but I soon returned to the job.

During one of these stays in Roehampton, I had a surprise visit from our squadron commander, Major Carlton, who was still with RTR. He told me that on the day our tank was knocked out at Tobruk only his and one other tank in the squadron had come back out. It was not mentioned by either of us that we had stopped by another tank. I am sure he never knew. I felt very sorry when he told me news had come through that Second Lieutenant V. D. C. York had been promoted to Captain on that fateful day, and he never knew.

Major Carlton was compiling information for the RTR library. Just before I started to write this book I went to the tank museum's library to obtain photocopies of Major Carlton's reports. I also paid a visit to Sandhurst for a rehearsal of the officers' passing out parade. After the parade, I went into the chapel, where there is a large book in a glass case. The book is a record of all officers who went through Sandhurst and had been killed. The Chaplain opened the case and looked up in the book and found Captain V. D. C. York, Middle East, 1941. The Chaplain kindly provided me with a photocopy of that page.

Unfortunately, I was more in Roehampton than at the job. Mr Randall asked me to speak at the Perrymount Cinema for the Red Cross. Just before I started my speech a BBC film was shown of the *Newfoundland* ship steaming out of the fog into port with Vera Lynn singing the 'White Cliffs of Dover', although of course it was not Dover but Avonmouth.

I believe it was in 1943 or 1944 that the Disability Act was going to be made law in the January. In December an engineer on the Electricity Board was in Electra House. I had just finished on the switchboard and was walking down the passage when he shouted to me to stop. I was on my two sticks and I did not take any notice, but when he shouted the second time I turned round and asked him if he had lost his dog! He came up to me and I threatened to hit him with one of my sticks. I

112

realised that this was being done so that they would have an excuse to sack me, which they did.

I had been thinking of getting a job outside again. The War Pension Depot had made me special boots, which I found a great help although they were very heavy. Just after I left the Electricity company, I saw a job advertised by a mushroom firm who had a farm at Noah's Ark Lane in Lindfield. The job was for a maintenance engineer, preferably war-disabled. The Disability Act, that was to come in force in January, meant that firms employing seven or more staff must employ one disabled in every seven. I applied for the job, and out of several others who applied got it. The work meant driving the van. This was the first time I had driven since my disability. The mushroom farm was run by a firm called Sparks from Worthing. There were eight mushroom houses. The houses were kept in partial darkness and all the work was carried out by lead lamps. The factory employed about 10 men and 30 to 40 girls. The girls worked in the houses most of the time but sometimes in the nursery behind the sheds, which grew lettuce and rhubarb.

My job was mainly electrical maintenance and taking the mushrooms to Haywards Heath station each evening. When there was a railway porters strike, I took the mushrooms from Lindfield to Covent Garden market, usually about 1,000 lbs each time. While at Covent Garden I would be asked to transport mushrooms left at Victoria station for other firms, for which they paid me. This strike went on for about two weeks. It was soon after I had been working for Sparks that they were bought out by Filmer Brothers from London. Filmers owned a factory in Clerkenwell making cardboard boxes. There were three brothers, and they had never been involved in mushrooms before. Each one of the brothers took over a department. One looked after finance and staff, the second looked after the mushroom houses. The eight houses were worked on rotation. There would be one house in which mushrooms were breaking on a first flush for picking, the next house mushrooms would have been picked for about two weeks and were now breaking out on a second flush, the third house would be coming to an end, and the rest of the houses were being prepared for another

113

turn of the cycle. The other brother, Jack, was a very clever engineer and I felt lucky that I worked with him. He was converting the electricity from 230 volts AC to 120 volts DC for safety in the houses for the girls with their lead lamps working in damp conditions.

I decided not to tell anyone about my disabilities. I made myself a golden rule never to talk about any of my war experiences to anyone. My thoughts were to get back to normal life. I was still living at Woodlands with my parents. I went back to Roehampton , mainly because my heel would not heal up. They tried a skin graft, but the skin died after a time.

I had another visitor while in Roehampton, this was Mr York, Yorkee's father. He had not come to terms with his son having been killed and wanted a first-hand account of just what happened that day. I told him exactly everything that happened. When I told him about the German officer sorting the wounded from those killed, Mr York asked if the officer had examined the bodies, to which I replied no, but as the officer was a medical man and owing to the concentrated gunfire in that area, I was certain he only left those killed. Mr York had an idea his son might be alive, living with the Bedouin in the desert. I assured him the Bedouin were never in that area and would only be found much further south in the desert. I never knew if he accepted my account or not. I believe it was through Major Carlton that Mr York found out where I was.

I did not want to be away from the job for too long. I was enjoying the work and felt I was getting back into civilian life very well. As bacon and pork were on ration, the Filmer brothers decided to start a pig club. A chap who worked there was interested in pigs, and he agreed to look after them. I was taken into the club, and altogether there were six of us: the three brothers, Jessie White, who would be looking after them, the foreman and myself. Jessie and I built the pig sties. We had all put some money in to start the club. We bought two small pigs to start with. When these became a certain age, we bought two more and then another two. When the first two were ready to be killed, it was my job to transport the pigs to a firm called Harris at Southampton. I was given a problem because petrol was on

114

ration. There were two colours for petrol then, white and red; white was for private use, and red was for commercial use only. I was doing these trips illegally, because the pig club was a private club and I was running on red petrol. The Filmers assured me they would cover me if anything happened. I took the first two pigs to the slaughterhouse at Southampton. It was usual to have one pig killed and returned as bacon and the other as pork, although this could vary according to our instructions.

Coming back from Southampton one very hot summer's day, I was stopped for speeding. In the back of the van I had three sides of bacon and one side of pork. I thought the policeman would ask to look in the back and also ask why I was so far from Lindfield, but he did not and seemed interested only in summonsing me. Filmers paid my fine. We were very lucky to get away so lightly.

The pig club became a great success. We were never short of bacon or pork. I also became more interested in mushroom growing. At Woodlands there was a stable which was not used for anything important, so I asked my parents if I could have it to grow some mushrooms in, and this they agreed to. I went to Frank Willet, who had a scrapyard next to the mushroom factory, and bought up about 20 single iron beds which I fixed up in the stables, three tiers high. I also purchased an old donkey boiler which I fitted into the stable with heating pipes. I got in touch with a stable in Epsom, as the best manure for growing mushrooms is horse manure. I ordered the amount I required, and this was delivered to Woodlands. I carried out all the work, turning the manure and putting this into the iron bedsteads about 9 inches deep, digging and sterilising the casing soil and planting the mushroom spores. After about five weeks I had my first flush of mushrooms. I started picking, and within a day or two I was taking baskets with about 5 lbs of mushrooms in each one round to the shops in Haywards Heath. Soon I realised there were far too many for the shops to take, so I started to send them up by train to a firm called Munros in Covent Garden. This went on for some weeks. Some days I was sending 20 lbs a day and was paid a pound per pound. The whole thing proved a great success. I asked my parents if I could build a shed to

115

grow more, but they refused for fear of being moved out, and this proved the end of my mushroom escapade.

At the Lindfield factory I started courting Doris King, who lived in Sunte Avenue, Lindfield. Doris was a very attractive girl, very slim, weighing only about eight stones and being five feet eight inches tall. Her hobby was ice-skating, which she was very good at. I went down to Brighton ice rink several times to watch her in action. Doris came from a family of nine, and her mother suffered with very bad asthma although only 45 years old. It seemed to me at the time when we met, her mother had been ill for a long time and Doris was looking after the family. Ice-skating was her only pleasure. She enjoyed a brandy and orange when we were out for an evening, and we both enjoyed country and western music and the Saturday evenings at the Hippodrome in Brighton. We also went to the cinema quite often. Whenever we wanted to go out we had to arrange for one of Doris's aunties to look after the children, and so we would never stay out too late. Doris's father was known in Lindfield as Squib and was a fairly heavy beer drinker. At the time when I started to go out with Doris, three of the youngest in the family were still going to school.

It was a night in June 1944 that I was woken by a very strange noise of an aircraft. My sister, who was living back home, came to my bedroom because of this strange noise. We looked out of the window to see what we thought was an aircraft on fire. It came over Haywards Heath and was flying in the direction of Cuckfield. We learnt later that it was something we were going to see a lot of in the near future – flying bombs.

These increased each night and day. One morning there were several passing overhead when a Spitfire manoeuvred his wing under the flying bomb, or doodlebug as we called them, and it fell in the corner of Franklands Wood just over the back of Woodlands. My mother had put two milk bottles on the back doorstep. We never saw any sign of those bottles again. I was outside and went flat on the ground when the blast went over the top of me. It was a Polish pilot who had brought it down. He came along several days later to see the damage. There were no houses then, as Franklands Village had not been built.

I now had to go to Hawkenbury at Tunbridge Wells for army medicals every three months. I would bus up, and after leaving the bus at Hawkenbury there were about 500 yards to walk from the road into the centre. All around were barrage balloons in the air on wire cables, the idea being that doodlebugs would hit the cable and be brought down. Most of the doodlebugs were heading for London and, of course, it was better that they be brought down in the country rather than on the capital.

One day, I was walking up to the medical centre when a doodlebug caught on one of the cables and came down in a ditch about 100 yards from where I was lying on the ground, and it did not explode. I lay for some time until the army disposal unit arrived and gave me the all clear to go into the centre. If it had exploded there would not have been a medical centre left, and again I was very lucky!

The flying bomb was like a small aircraft, 26 feet long with a wing span of 16 feet and a total weight of 2 tons, including 1,800 lbs of explosive. It flew at about 3,000 feet with a speed of 375 mph and it was designed to reach London and then the fuel would run out. It exploded when it hit the ground.

The war finally ended on 2 September 1945.

11

Marriage

I had been courting Doris for about 18 months. My mother would not accept Doris in the house at Woodlands, and I have always believed that the reason Doris was not welcome was my mother's fear of me getting married. The situation at that time was that my father was quite a heavy drinker and my mother was always lending him money. I enjoyed a drink but was more interested in wireless and mechanical things. Woodlands had deteriorated as a smallholding, mainly because my father would not re-invest money back into the business or let my mother do so. He would rather take it to the pub. I also suspected that as my brother was living in nearby Bentswood Road with a small family, he was also asking mother for money.

Doris and I had plans to get married and we were saving together. I had not been back in hospital for some time and had settled down very well. I enjoyed the work with Jack at the factory as it was now mainly experimental work to create different atmospheres in the mushroom houses. Some of the ideas worked well and the mushroom output was increased by large amounts. One morning in early 1946, Doris did not turn up for work. The news came later that morning that her mother had died. I went to her house that day and helped her the best I could. It soon became clear that Doris was being mother to the family and had to give up her job. After the funeral I decided that perhaps the best thing for us was to get married and I would move into Oak Cottage, Doris's home. There was an older sister, Olive, who was married and lived in Haywards Heath.

118

Doris was worried more about her father who, as we knew, was a heavy drinker.

Her father was working in London as a foreman on building work repairing bomb-damaged houses. He travelled by lorry each day and was then earning very good wages. We had a meeting, Squib, Doris and myself. Squib said that if we got married and lived there at Oak Cottage he would pay all the bills. He owned the cottage so there was no rent or mortgage, and so this was all agreed. We made arrangements to get married at the Registry Office. Doris had an aunt Gert who lived two doors from Oak Cottage and who agreed to come as witness along with Squib. My parents would not come but I expected they would be upset as they would be losing the money I had paid them each week.

The marriage was arranged for 8 June 1946. The family we had agreed to look after were Irene, Doris's younger sister, who was still going to school, Leslie, the youngest brother, and Jeffrey, who were both still at school, and Kenny, who had just left school and was training to be an engine driver on the railway. The other older brothers and sisters were either married or living away from home. Because of the younger brothers and sisters we could not stay away after we married, and so we hired a car for the weekend so we could get out for days. Aunt Gert would look after the family during the days we were away.

I made arrangements with a garage in Balcombe to hire a car for three days. The owner was called Shenley. It was £2 a day to hire. He asked me how I was going to get to Balcombe to pick the car up on the Saturday morning. I said the same way as I had come to make the arrangements – on my cycle. I agreed then on £5 deposit and my cycle to be left with him. I did not see the car at that time, as it was out on hire. As this was in the early days of car hire, at that time there were very few places where one could hire a car.

We also arranged for a small reception at Doris's home. On the morning of our wedding I cycled to Balcombe to pick up the car. Shenley had it all ready and I paid him the money. He opened the door for me to get in, and the handle came off. I complained about the state of the car, and he told me it had not

119

been brought back the night before so he could have had it serviced and cleaned out, and also he had been told that it had been seen being used for moving house. He fixed the handle and I drove off. I was pleased that I had gone up early, as it would give me time to clean it out before I went over to pick up Doris and her dad and aunt. It was a very old car, and when it was being driven I had to pump the oil when the pressure got too low. It was a 'square Jane' and was four doors with a sun roof. The bonnet was of a lift-up type with two catches on each side.

The wedding was not until 12 o'clock, so I had good time to clean it out and wash it. I also took some tools; I had a feeling I might need them. It now became a very hot day so I was pleased to have the sun roof open. I went over to Oak Cottage and picked up Doris, aunt Gert and Squib. I drove to the Registry Office, which was next to the main Post Office in Boltro Road, and we were married and I paid 7/6d to the Registrar. Aunt Gert was first outside, and as we got into the car she threw confetti over us. I thought perhaps, at the last minute, someone from my family might turn up, but no one did. We had our small reception, and I was surprised how many of Doris's relatives were there and also that most of them lived in Sunte Avenue.

We set off on our own late that afternoon. I headed for Brighton, and we were about to go up Clayton Hill when there was a loud bang. The whole bonnet had taken off on its own and crashed in the road behind us. When I was fitting it back on I noticed that the springs in the four side slips holding the bonnet down were broken and had been tied with string.

We had just arrived in London Road in Brighton when, because it had been so hot, a storm started. I tried to close the sunroof, but it would not move. With the torrential rain, the car was starting to flood inside. We got out and stood in a shop doorway until the storm was over. We then carried on in a wet car to Littlehampton, where we stopped and had an evening meal while the car was drying out. We arrived back at Oak Cottage late that evening, and we never again got to go out on our own. The next day, Sunday, was spent taking the younger brothers and sisters out for rides. I went back to work on

Monday, and we settled down to start our married life bringing up a ready-made family.

Within a few months Leslie left school and started work as an errand boy. Rene and Jeffrey were due to leave within the next year or two. My shoe repairing experience now came in very handy, and I repaired all the shoes at Oak Cottage.

It was in November that I received notice from the War Pension department that my disability pension was to be reduced from 30 per cent to 20 per cent; this meant that I would only receive 20 per cent for the next 12 months, and then receive a final sum of £100, and that would be the end of my pension. Through the British Legion I gave notice of appeal. The man who was dealing with it left the British Legion and no one had filled in the job until nine months after I had lodged the appeal. Although I had given the Legion my defence, they had done nothing about it. As it happened, the day my appeal was to be heard in London I was back in Roehampton, and the day before the appeal, I had an operation to remove some more shrapnel from my leg. They asked me at Roehampton if I would agree to go to the tribunal on a stretcher, to which I agreed. They phoned the tribunal to say I would be attending on the stretcher and the answer was not to bring me but my pension would be put back to 30 per cent!

After a time, we found Squib was not keeping to the agreement and not paying the bills. It became a worry for Doris, and so from time to time we took money from our savings to pay bills. When most of our savings were gone, we decided to give up living at Oak Cottage. Olive had separated from her husband, Cath had decided to come back home to live, and Rene and Jeffrey had now left school. During the time we lived in Oak Cottage I had also been involved in repairing and rebuilding old bicycles. I had learnt a lot from Les when I worked for Dinnages about bicycles. I bought up old ones, rebuilt them and advertised them in our local paper, the *Mid-Sussex Times*. Money which we made from this was put with our savings, which was in turn being used to pay the bills.

My sister at this time was living in Bentswood Crescent, Haywards Heath, in a council house. They offered us the front two rooms to live in until we could find a place of our own. We moved into the Crescent and did not feel guilty at leaving Oak Cottage. We settled down very well with my sister and Fred, my brother-in-law. He had been a coal miner in Durham, but when the pits started to close had come south to find work. He never settled in one job for very long and was out of work when we moved in with them. We were not short of bacon or pork, although in the hot weather we were giving some away, as in those days there were no refrigerators or freezers to keep food in.

It was during 1947 that my heel was giving me a lot of trouble and I had to go back into Roehampton for another skin graft. They tried several, but the skin kept dying. I was able to come home at weekends on crutches. As it happened, the surgeon who was working on my heel lived in Three Bridges, and when he came down by car he was kind enough to bring me home, Three Bridges being only a few miles from Haywards Heath, and he also picked me up on Monday mornings. It was during this time that Doris became pregnant. They investigated the reason why the skin grafts kept dying, and found there was a diseased bone. I had been having a graft every two weeks and the skin was being taken from my behind, which hardly had any skin left on it. I had an operation to remove the diseased parts and came home for a break.

When I got home I was given a shock. Someone had reported to the Housing Manager that we were living in a council house and my sister had not asked permission from the Housing Manager, Mr Staines, to allow us to lodge there. It was late in the evening when I was told that Mr Staines had called to see my sister and Doris. They explained the position to him, that I was back in Roehampton, but he ignored anything they said and told Doris to get out within the next week. The next morning, I walked on my crutches from the Crescent to Colwell Close, where Mr Staines lived, and caught him before he had his eyes open. When I explained who I was and asked him to give us time so that I could find somewhere for Doris, he refused to listen to me and insisted Doris must be out within a week. I could not believe what I was hearing from this man. I agreed that my

122

sister had overlooked the rules about this, but all I was asking was for time to get out. When I realised what kind of specimen of a man I was dealing with, I told him a lot of things he never knew about himself! I was to clash with him again later in life.

I went that same day to see my doctor, Dr Dodd in Gander Hill. There was no appointment in those days. One would take a turn as one arrived. This was the second time I had seen Dr Dodd. He listened to what I told him and wrote a letter while I was there and told me to take it to the Housing Manager's office. I then went back to Roehampton and explained what had happened at home, and they postponed any further treatment for a week so I could go home to sort things out. After I was back home about three days, we had a letter from the council to say we had been allocated a semi-detached chalet bungalow in America Lane. It had just been built, and we could move in the following Monday. I went over to thank Dr Dodd and at the same time I mentioned my problem with bleeding piles, only to discover that he suffered from the same thing. I told him I had had two operations in Epsom Hospital which had made things worse, and he agreed that they would have been better left alone. I will never know what he put in the letter to the Council, but they certainly moved very quickly. Staines lost his job very soon after this as Housing Manager and became the Sanitary Inspector!

I was pleased to be home to help Doris. We did not have a lot of furniture, but at last we were on our own. Doris settled in and I went back to Roehampton, where I had more skin grafts which took all right, and for the first time my heel healed up and since then has not given me any more trouble. I was never given any pension for the heel.

On 22 April 1948, we had a baby girl, Valerie, who was born at the old Cuckfield Hospital; during the time I was still in Roehampton, so I had not seen the baby. I had some more shrapnel removed and for some time was confined to bed. Money was very short, and it was about two months before Doris could bring Valerie up to Roehampton for me to see her for the first time.

I came back home and went back to work at the mushroom

factory. Another chap was driving the van and wanted to carry on doing so, which to me seemed fair enough. I still had the maintenance work. After a time, I felt that I needed to get back into the domestic side of the electrical world and I applied to a firm called Horace Hilton, who were situated in Sussex Square in Haywards Heath, to see if there was a vacancy. Hiltons had an ironmongers shop facing onto Sussex Square, and to the rear were workshops where they employed about 12 electricians and mates and also about the same number of plumbers and their mates. The workshop carried out all kinds of repairs to household appliances, such as kettles and electric irons, in fact anything that was repairable. I was given an interview with a man called Jack Hamilton who, at that time, was the electrical fore-man. He explained to me that if taken on, I would be expected to help out in other departments, and this, I said, was what I was hoping to do. He asked if I would be able to fit a new bottom to a tin kettle, but I explained that I had not done this before. He then produced a tin kettle, some tin and the necessary flux, sol-der and cleaning material to carry out the job, and left me in the workshop to see what I could do. In about half an hour I took the kettle with a new bottom to him. He boiled it up and remarked that it was a good first effort. I got the job, gave a week's notice at the mushroom factory and started with Hiltons.

Mr Hilton had two sons, Keith and John, who both worked in the business. Keith looked after the shop and John was in con-trol of the finances. Mr Hilton lived in a detached house in Wivelsfield Road with a very large garden. I now felt I was at long last settling into a normal life with a good job. In 1949 we had a son, Raymond. The bungalow had only one bedroom on the ground floor and a box room on the first floor. We had our name down for a larger house, but at that time there was a very large housing list.

My second own transport was a secondhand autocycle which had a 50cc engine. Having the cycle helped me a lot, and I used it to go out to the jobs I was given. I was still going to Hawkenbury at Tunbridge Wells for medical checks and went a number of times on the autocycle.

The plumbing foreman at Hiltons was Ted Westlake, and

when the electrical work had temporarily slowed down, I was asked to help out on the plumbing side. A chap called Mr Butcher from Eastern Road, Lindfield, was perhaps one of the best plumbers employed at Hiltons, and he had just started a very large plumbing and heating job at Cragwood, a large house in Horsted Keynes, about six miles from Haywards Heath, and opposite what was then known as the Horsted Keynes Jam Factory. I was asked to go with this plumber (nicknamed Wally), and we used to catch a bus about 7 a.m. from Lindfield to a point just before the bus got into Horsted Keynes and then walk about a mile to Cragwood. I never let anyone know about my leg, although Mr Hilton knew I was registered disabled. I decided not to say too much about it. Wally and myself got on very well, and I learnt a lot about plumbing. In those days it was mainly iron and lead work, and it was very heavy work compared with present-day plumbing.

Whenever a special job had to be carried out, Wally would have to leave the job at Cragwood. Sometimes I carried on the work myself while Wally was away. On one occasion we were told to be at the workshop on a certain morning. Ted Westlake instructed us that we were to be at a house off the Brighton Road to seal down a coffin. You will recall I mentioned earlier Mr Kleinwort and his long beard. He was being buried in a lead coffin, and our job was to solder the lid. My job was to hold the lid down tight while Wally ran the solder round with a blow lamp. Wally was worried that, because of the heat, he would set the beard alight. In fact, as there were only two of us in the room, Wally said it would be better if I sat on the lid to keep it really tight. This worked very well.

My sister had moved out of Bentswood Crescent and had gone back to live at Woodlands with our parents. She had two children at that time and was expecting another. My parents would not agree to her having the baby at Woodlands, so Doris and I agreed to let her stay at our home in America Lane to have the baby. Fred, her husband, did not stay with us. The night she had the baby Doris and I were responsible. I went for the nurse and we were up all that night and my sister had her third girl,

Mary. The nurse called in Dr Kilpack, and the next morning he confirmed that all was fine with my sister and the baby. Within a couple of days she went back to Woodlands.

After a couple of years working with Wally, I was quite capable of carrying out plumbing work on my own. It was about this time that copper tube for use in plumbing came onto the market. This was something new to everyone in plumbing work, so I felt now that I was on the same level with everyone else. It was so easy to work with after threading iron pipes. The next thing to come into plumbing was plastic pipe work, and these two things took a lot of the heavy work out of plumbing. I was beginning to think again about one day working for myself. The knowledge I was accumulating with Hiltons would put me on the right road. I was taken off the plumbing side because there was a road being built down Victoria Road, connecting with Eastern Road down to Woodlands. There were 16 three-bedroomed houses being built in Victoria Road and at the back of the road a new school, with an entrance from the lower end of Eastern Road and another new road, North Road. Hiltons had the contract to wire the 16 houses, and I was given the job to carry out the electrical wiring for these. Hiltons took on a young man who was keen on learning about electrical work: his name was Tom Hamid, and he was to be my mate for the next few years. We became very good friends. Tom was about 20 and had come from Bristol, where he had worked as a prison warder.

The road down to Victoria Road was now built, and I started the wiring on the new houses. Tom was working with me, and also I was given an apprentice. We started at the beginning of a very bad winter, 1949. Although my parents were still living in Woodlands, I did not go in very much. I took my flask and sandwiches each day and was quite happy to sit with everyone else, however cold it was. I was still doing any spare-time work I could get. One Monday morning I had to see Mr Hilton in his office, and he warned me that if I did not stop doing electrical or plumbing work in my spare time I would be sacked, as it was against the law. I told him I would look for something else in my spare time, but I never did! It was still very much in my mind to work for myself.

While I was working on the Victoria Road houses we received a letter from the Housing Department to say we had been allocated one of the houses I was working on. It was next door to Jenner's bungalow. Although Mrs Jenner had died, Mr Jenner and the daughter, Mary, were still living there. These houses were expected to be finished by 1950. The only disappointment I had was that I could not get a drive in or build a garage, but as these were things still in my mind and yet to come, I would sort that out later. The main thing at the moment was room for the children.

We moved to Victoria Road during the summer of 1950. The new school was now open and the playground came up to our back garden. Soon after moving there I was again told to see Mr Hilton, and this time Keith and John were also in the office. It was because I was doing spare-time work. I told Mr Hilton it was well known that he had come to Haywards Heath on a bus with a toolbox and a shilling in his pocket and had married and worked hard to start a business and bring up his family, and he agreed with me about that, and I said that that was all I was trying to do. He asked me if I could not do something else apart from the work I was carrying out for him, but I told him that was all I knew. He then suggested gardening, of which I knew nothing. He offered me work at his house in Wivelsfield Road and to do some hedge cutting, and this I agreed to do.

When I went there on the following Saturday afternoon, I found the hedge to be cut was 12 feet high, After I had cut it, which took several evenings, he asked me to carry out other jobs in the garden. I spent several evenings and Saturday afternoon working there. Mr Hilton always had a cup of tea on Saturdays after lunch and before going back to the shop. I had been working in his garden for seven weeks, and there had been no mention of pay. I decided the time had come to ask him and, while he was on the terrace one Saturday, I mentioned it to him, and he told me he thought I had been putting it on my time sheet each week. I had, up to then, about 80 hours overtime, so I put this on my next time sheet and received what was then a little windfall.

In 1951 we had another boy, Dennis. Valerie, the eldest, was

127

not due to start school for another year. Although we lived only 100 yards from my mother, she seldom came up to see us and Doris was not very happy when she did come. There was no love lost between Doris and my parents. We never rowed with them, but kept ourselves apart as much as possible.

Mary Jenner, at 65, decided to get married and had a white wedding. Her father died soon after the wedding, and very soon after that her husband died. This left Mary on her own. Losing her father and husband in so short a time was bad enough, but the solicitor dealt another blow when he told her that the bungalow and all its contents had been left, by her father, to some of his relations in Devon. He also told her that if there was any cash in the bungalow to take it into his office. She came to Doris and myself for advice, and we told her not take any money into the office. She said there was only £80 and felt she should hand it in, which she did. However, the will was not dated and everything eventually went to Mary. Although the relations had been up from Devon and taken a lot of the furniture, they had to return it.

Mary decided to take a mortgage on the bungalow and asked me to carry out repairs and redecoration, and I started work. Nothing had ever been done in the bungalow since it had been built, so I had plenty of work on my hands. In two of the bedrooms the lino had turned to dust under the beds. I had to throw buckets of water across the floors to lay the dust. The only good thing about the job was that it was next door. At this time Mary was still working for the Lindfield Laundry, which was situated at the end of Gravelye Lane. When I had completed the work, Mary retired from the laundry and took a job as a lollipop lady in Franklynn Road, and it was while doing this job that she was hit by a car and killed.

Tom and his wife used to come down to visit my home, but we did not get on too well with his wife. We found her very mean and dominating. One day Tom did not turn up for work, so I called in to his house and no one knew where he was. I found him later that morning, as he had been seen walking towards Lindfield, on the common, sitting on a seat very upset. They were living in two rooms with her parents, who were

128

fairly well-off. Tom told me he was saving the money he earned with our-spare time work to buy a wooden shed to use as a workshop. When he got home the day before, the parents had bought the shed. Tom told me he had nothing he felt was his own because of her parents, and his wife had told him everything they had belonged to her. They had one boy, but Tom, because they would not allow him to be independent, eventually divorced her and went into lodgings.

Tom and myself, because of our interest in wireless and now television, had both become friendly with another chap called Norman Hobbs who had the same interest. Tom was lodging in Ashenground Road, and the three of us spent many evenings together repairing wirelesses. I met Norman's father on a job I was working on for Hiltons. His father was a first-class carpenter who specialised in working with oak timber. Norman, Tom and myself pooled our knowledge and problems together. Norman was a very clever chap with televisions and opened a shop in Sussex Road. The strange thing about Norman was he had no interest in driving. Soon after he opened the shop he had a van and driver, who was also very good in the electrical world, and used to drive Norman around. Tom met a girl from Jersey, and they got married and he moved out there. He started his own business hiring out jukeboxes to cafés and restaurants and became very successful. When they could spare a weekend they would fly out to Gatwick, hire a car and stay with us. We would make up a bed for them on the floor. I did not hear from Tom for quite a while, then one day his wife arrived to tell us Tom had died from cancer. He had asked her not to let us know anything about it when he was in hospital, but to come to see us after he had died. This was a very sad blow to Doris and me, as Tom had always been a true friend.

A hotel in Haywards Heath, the Birch, was advertising for a maintenance engineer, so I went to see the owner, a Commander Harris. The wage would be better than Hiltons, but the main thing to me was I would be working on my own. I thought this would be useful for the next few years until the children became older, and I could then go out on my own. Commander Harris, who I shall now refer to by his christian name, Richard, because he had always had Hiltons do his work, went to see Mr Hilton, who told me if I went to the hotel to work and was not happy, there would always be a job for me at Hiltons.

I started work for Richard and his wife. There·was a large swimming pool, which, during the summer, was open to the public. Richard suffered with a very bad heart and moved about the grounds of the hotel in an electrical invalid chair. The filtration system to the pool was very old and needed a lot of work to bring it up to a reasonable standard. The electrical work and plumbing in the hotel were in very bad condition and needed updating. Richard explained to me that money was very short and the hotel had always been on an overdraft. He came to me soon after I had started because the sewer drain was blocked. The hotel at that time had its own sewerage system in a wood below a farm which also belonged to the hotel. The hotel was originally a private house, built in 1912, and the sewerage system had never been altered. I told Richard that if he would provide me with replacement parts for the sewerage beds and for the pool's filtration plant, I would carry out the work to bring these systems up to date. All this work I carried out over time. This was giving me confidence in carrying out larger jobs on my own.

Over the next couple of years Richard's health deteriorated very fast. Mrs Harris was now running the hotel on her own. It was in 1952 that Richard told me the hotel was at last out of the red and showing a profit. He asked if I would take over running the swimming pool that summer, and I agreed, provided I had another maintenance man to help with the larger jobs.

I was able to employ two attendants for the pool. There was a tea hut down by the pool, and Doris brought all the children up late afternoons, and they all learnt to swim. We could have tea, and we spent a lot of time there. As it was the only swimming pool in the area at that time we could, on a good summer's day, bring in 300 or more swimmers. For this I would get one penny on every ticket purchased. We had several celebrities who called in to the hotel: Vera Lynn was very often there at the pool in the afternoon, Jimmy Edwards always called in on New Year's Eve for a free drink at the staff party given by Richard, when all the drinks were free, and Bill Owen was there after doing a cabaret act in the evening.

The swimming pool was drained out in early spring for maintenance and painting, and was refilled from mains water through a special meter. It took thousands of gallons of water to refill and more to replenish throughout the season.

The floor in the kitchen had to be re-tiled, and Richard arranged for a tiling firm to carry out the work, mainly at night as the staff were working during the day and evenings. I was asked to do certain jobs in the kitchen in preparation for the tiling, and one of the jobs was to fit a manhole cover over a well. This would be a special cover which could be tiled but also lifted out for access to the well. I became interested in this well and decided to find out more about it. When I worked for Hiltons, we had put a Sumo electrical pump down a well at the Holy Cross convent, which was at the end of Bolnore Road. This pump was shaped very much like a torpedo, about six inches in diameter and it was screwed onto 20-foot lengths of two-inch galvanised pipes and lowered down into the well. The electrical cables were strapped to the pipework and this was fixed to the side of the well. I also knew of another one being fixed down a well for a laundry in Franklynn Road, and I remembered that some of the houses along Lewes Road when I was a boy had windmill pumps in their gardens, pumping up water from an underground river.

In one of the old cottages in Victoria Road lived two brothers, Harry and Sid Stemp. When I first moved into Woodlands I could just remember their father, a very short little man who always smoked one-penny clay pipes, which were white in colour and would only last for one day. The father died soon after we moved in, when I was about 14 and he was about 72. He would have started work in about 1874 and was a well digger. At this time Harry had died but Sid was still alive, so I went to have a talk with him about the wells. It so happened that his father had been in charge of the excavation of this same well when the house was built. It was Sid who told me there was an underground river flowing from Scaynes Hill through under Lewes Road, Franklynn Road and Bolnore Road, and that when

Birch House was built there was a pump down in the well. I felt sure it was still there. The next thing was to lower a lamp down to 100 feet. I could see the river flowing through, with ferns and green plants growing on the sides, and I also found there was a sump at about another 20 feet. I contacted a laboratory in Brighton, and they would test the water provided I could get it to them within a certain time from taking the sample. This was done, and it was reported that there was a slight contamination which should clear after a turn-over of a few million gallons. I laid in two-inch by two-inch galvanised pipes and cable from the top of the well through under the kitchen floor to a passage, ready to put a pump down. I then completed the rest of the man-hole cover. Unfortunately, the well was never used as Richard's health deteriorated, but I feel convinced that it would have been a sound investment at that time. Richard was now confined to his bedroom, and I worked with Mrs Harris.

Doris and I decided to take the children down to Devon to stay in bed and breakfast and have a few days at the seaside. Neither Doris nor myself cared for the seaside, but in fairness to the children, they enjoyed it. On the way down and when we arrived in Devon, it rained hard the whole time. The seaside was out of the question, so we decided to carry on through to Wales, staying at farms. The children enjoyed the farms and the animals, even though it rained every day. On the way back I decided to stop in Worcester overnight to see if I could find Bill Meadows, our tank driver. I remembered part of his address. We booked in for B & B and then I went out to find him, which I did. We had a long chat about old times, and I asked about the boy who we heard was born while we listened to the news from our tank radio. He was now about 12 years old. I took Doris to meet Bill and his wife the next morning before we left, but I have not seen him again.

I was still interested in wireless and television, and decided to build my own television. The only television I knew of was a console HMV that belonged to Richard and Mrs Harris. It was a very large set comprising an auto record player, radio and 12-inch television. I understand this was the first television to be installed in Haywards Heath. No one in our local area had television, and I could not afford to buy everything needed at one time, so I purchased a few components whenever we could spare the money. Doris said I was mad, as it would never work.

The bookstall at the Haywards Heath railway station did not open on Sundays, and the Sunday papers were sold by a man who I knew through my brother, who lived near him. He had to give up the Sunday job owing to ill health, and I was asked if I would take this on, which involved being up at the station all day on Sunday from 5 a.m. until 9 p.m. I took this job. I had a wooden trestle table to lay out the papers. These arrived by a train known as the paper train, which came down from London and arrived at Haywards Heath at about 5 a.m. I would buy the papers by the quire, which was 24 papers to a quire, from an old schoolfriend of mine, Tom Rawlings, whose father had a shop in Wivelsfield Road. There was a large family of Rawlings, and all the children had to work in the shop or around the yard, which sold coal. Tom had to deal with the papers. This job went on for about two years and then the bookstall opened on Sundays. On a good day I could earn £5 or more, which was about half a week's wages.

The coronation of Queen Elizabeth II was to be on 2 June 1953. Street parties were being arranged for all the children, and it was to be a public holiday. I had been building the television for about 18 months as I could only spare about one evening a week after the children had gone to bed, and, as I did not have a workshop, I would work on the kitchen table. The coronation was going to be televised, and I hoped to finish it in time so we could watch it (or Doris would be proved right). The most expensive part was the tube. I asked Norman and another friend, who had a radio shop in Wivelsfield, Guy Austen, who managed to get hold of a 9-inch, secondhand tube, which he felt sure would still work. If it worked I would pay him £10, which was far more than one week's wages. I told Guy I had almost completed building my own set and would not be sure, if it did not work, whether it was my set or his tube. He had a set in the shop with a 9-inch tube and kindly changed the tubes over for me, to be sure it would be all right. I took a gamble and paid

133

him the £10. When I had completed the set I put up a temporary aerial. Doris would not stay in the room the first time I switched the set on. All that happened was a large cloud of smoke went up. It was two resistors which had burnt out because I had wired them incorrectly. After several adjustments I was receiving a very good picture. Just before the coronation, although I had not put the set into a cabinet, Doris thought it would be nice to have all the children in the road in to watch the coronation. She was helping with the street party, and also my mother helped. We moved some of the furniture out and borrowed some long wooden seats from the school for the party, and we put some in our front room for the children to sit on.

It was a lovely summer's day for the coronation, and our front room was packed with children and grown-ups. Although we had to keep the curtains drawn, it was a perfect day. The television worked well for the next three years, and a friend who had done me a favour said he would like to have it as I was buying a new one.

I still had my autocycle but we decided to get a secondhand car, although I knew we would have to leave it out on the road. At the same time I was looking for an older house which we might be able to buy. I was never happy paying rent. I bought a car in Lewes. It was a Flying Standard 12 and cost £85, which I took on hire purchase. However, I soon realised I had bought plenty of trouble. The big ends and pistons were badly worn. I had to strip down the engine and rebuild it and fit new kingpins, not at all easy with the car out on the road. Once the work was completed, it was quite a large car for the family, and we kept it for several years.

My sister and family were now living in Bentswood Road. I went down to sweep a chimney for her as Fred, her husband, would not do anything like that. Everyone had coal fires in those days. While I was talking to her, she was saying how much they would like to live in one of the houses like I had in Victoria Road. I talked to Doris about changing over, provided I had enough width to get a drive in. It was so overgrown between the neighbours it was difficult to tell, so I went down to measure, and it was practicable to get a drive up to the back of the house as there was plenty of garden, which was also over-grown. My sister would make the change, and I went to the Council to check that this would be all right and would I be able to buy the council house?

We would change over, and once I had paid one week's rent I could buy it. This was agreed, and I bought 117 Bentswood Road for £940 over 15 years. Doris was upset as the rent was only 18s a week and we would be paying £1 10s a week repayment. I assured her we could do it.

I still went up to Hawkenbury for a medical examination once a year. Now we had the car I could take Doris and leave her in Tunbridge Wells shopping. Richard Harris passed away in 1957.

Doris became pregnant, and our third son, Richard, was born in 1958. Mrs Harris carried on the hotel for another year. It was during that last summer when, because it was so hot, we had our record number of visitors to the pool and tea grounds, that Mrs Harris sold the hotel to a man who, at that time, owned a large hotel on Brighton front. Mrs Harris invited him and his wife to come and stay for a month at the Birch before the signing over. This was the worst thing she could have done. They were the most horrible couple I had ever met. Within the first week, he carried on as if he owned the place. He had Mrs Harris in tears several times while he was there. I told him during the first week to keep out of my way. He spoke to everyone as if they were his employees. I was very pleased when Mrs Harris told me she had a friend who was a bookmaker in Brighton and London, called Harry Safron, and on the day of the signing Harry would be in the hotel and sitting in at the event. There were also some of Harry's employees who would be in the bar area if required.

During the last week Mrs Harris asked me if I would spend a couple of evenings burning up a lot of personal things of hers and Richard's. I was burning up a lot this one evening, when this man and his wife came along to see why there was a fire. At that moment I had just thrown on the fire some of Richard's 'Commander' uniforms from when he was in the Navy. She asked me to take them back off the fire, saying they could be used for stage plays. I refused, and she got a pole and was going to get them off herself. I struggled with her, and got the pole away and chased them away from the site. The next morning they both came to my workshop to inform me that when they took over the hotel on the coming Friday, the first thing they would do would be to consider whether I would still be employed, and she asked me, at least for the rest of the week, not to get on to her husband, as he was suffering from a bad heart. I thanked them both for letting me know their position, and I informed them that on the Friday, if the hotel was signed over to them, I would be driving out at the same time with my cards and pay, and as for his bad heart, I said I would hope that by the time I finished with him he would not be there on the Friday to sign! That was, I believe, the last time I spoke to either of them, as they avoided me for the rest of that week.

12

Self-employed

I had already decided, from the day I knew Mrs Harris was going to sell the hotel, that I would make the break and work for myself. Doris was very unhappy about the situation, and I knew it would be hard going as the children were very still very small. Richard had just been born; Dennis was six; Raymond was nine and Valerie ten. We had not been in Bentswood Road very long. If I felt it was not working, I was confident I could get a job. I sold the car and bought a Husky van. I also bought a small set of copper benders.

My first job was for a relation of Doris, Don Shergold in Petlands Road. They had a removal business, which was well known in Haywards Heath at that time. During the first year I was quite happy how things were going. A local chap, who was on his own decorating, came to me about estimating for a large job in Haywards Heath. It was a very large house which was to be made into two separate accommodations. Each side would have all new systems, including the electrical work. The owners would still be living in the house while the work was being done. I worked out an estimate and decided it would look better if it was typed out. I bought a cheap portable typewriter from Smiths in the town for £18. As I was working each day, I stayed up for two whole nights learning how to type with one finger. I completed the estimate and gave it to the decorator. Within a short time he told me he had signed a contract with the owners, who wanted the work started as soon as possible. He explained that my estimate had been satisfactory and the whole work

137

could start as soon as I could. I worked out a date and started. The decorator was painting a house opposite the one I was working in.

After a few weeks I approached him about some money. He said he would make arrangements with the owners to get some payment. I explained to him that, as the contractor, he was responsible to pay me, and not the owners. I did get some, but not all that I had requested. He then came to me and said that he had been let down by a builder and carpenter who were to be involved with the work. I knew of a builder and a carpenter, and they came to the rescue. After a few months I was having a lot of trouble with money. I had large bills from the wholesalers and could not get any from the contractor. I had myself been working up to 12 o'clock at night. The owners were very nice genuine people, and I did not feel it was right to involve them.

I decided to pull out of the job. I made several trips with my van, moving all my equipment. The owner must have realised something was wrong, and asked me why I was taking all my tools away. I told her I could not carry on without money. She then told me they had been paying the decorator every two weeks. When the owner got the contractor there, he said he would pay me when he decided to do so. I told them that until he did that I had no alternative but to leave the job. I sent the decorator my account made up to the time I left, but did not hear any more about it. Because of all the worry and working too hard, I became ill and was taken into Hurstwood Hospital.

I had to make up my mind whether to pack up on my own or carry on. Doris left it to me to decide, and I decided to carry on. My thoughts were that, if I could get over the financial side, I was quite confident about my work. I arranged an overdraft with the bank to help me out on the finance side. Through my solicitor and a barrister we eventually had the decorator in Brighton Court. I had a legal aid certificate but he did not, and so we settled at the gates to the court. I was quite happy. as I had covered myself and he had to pay all the costs. Then we went into court. I was more than happy when the judge dressed him down and told him what a fool he was. It also came out that he and his wife had taken a month's holiday and stayed in a hotel in Devon with my money. The judge made an order that he was to pay £20 a month. It took him several years to pay the money back.

After 18 months, I had started to do work on the house. Doris had a lot of good ideas, and we started to alter and modernise it as we would like it. My sister and Fred came down and remarked that they wished they had stayed and carried out alterations as we were doing. I remarked that I was talking to the lady next door and she would have liked one of the houses in Victoria Road. They then changed over with my neighbour, but had to pay another £1,500 more than we had paid. I knew then we had done the right thing in buying. It always surprised me that not many took up the Council's offer to buy.

Doris had an aunt Rose, who lived in Dorking, and one Sunday we decided to pay a visit. After lunch, I was talking to her uncle, Bert, when I happened to mention that our gunner, Dusty Miller, came from Dorking, but I had no idea of his address. He said that if I looked out of the window there was a row of terraced cottages, and in the second one from the left was a Mr Miller who, Bert thought, was in the tanks during the war. I decided to walk down and knock on the door. It was Dusty, our gunner. He invited me in, and we had a chat over old times. The next time we went to Dorking, I took Doris and introduced her to Dusty. We did not get back to Dorking for maybe a year or two. I went over to the cottage, only to learn that Dusty and family had emigrated to Australia.

The builder who had helped me out during my first year, Ted Duffy, was very busy, mainly building extensions on houses. There was a big demand about that time for the type of work. He gave me all the plumbing and heating and electrical work and was the only genuine builder I would work for. This work for Ted became my mainstay. Ted also had a decorator who carried out all his decorating, and his name was Den Horton, from Ardingly, a small village a few miles from Haywards Heath. Den was married and had two girls. We all became very friendly, and I would take Doris and the children to Ardingly to visit them, and sometimes they came to us.

Den and myself were working in the same room one day and,

during the conversation, I was saying to Den that I was very interested in flying. Den replied that he was also interested in the same thing. As we both felt we could not afford to take it up just at that time, we would both learn together. Later on, we did go up to Biggin Hill from time to time to watch the students learning.

During 1963, Valerie had left school and was training to be a nurse at the Cuckfield Hospital; Raymond had just left school and came to work with me. He had done so before he left school and had worked with me on Saturdays, and so was well advanced in plumbing by the time he left school. Dennis, who was now about 12, always said he wanted to go into the Navy. Richard had not yet started school.

One day, I was travelling down Western Road when I noticed a small open lorry stationary on the left hand side of the road. As I passed, I also noticed a man coming out of a gate towards the lorry, with a bin on his shoulder. I thought I recognised the face, so I stopped and walked back. As I was walking towards the lorry, the man was about to drive off when he saw me. He sat in the driving seat with his mouth open. It was as I had thought, Sergeant Beech from Fletching. He was collecting pig food for his farm. I reminded him about that pint of beer he promised me in the Burrell when we were in the desert at Fort Mechili. We met that evening in the Burrell and had more than one pint and a very long conversation. I have not seen him since.

13

Irish Connection

My sister was living on one side of us, but on the other side, in the house which was attached to our own, we had new neighbours. A few nights after they moved in, they had a housewarming party. Doris and I were in bed listening to the piano accordion being played, and wished we were joining in with them. It was obvious from the music they were Irish. The next day I was in the back garden when the neighbour came up to make an apology for the noise the night before. I told him how much we both enjoyed the music, and we got talking and when he realised we had four children he worried they had been kept awake. We assured him it did not worry them. We introduced ourselves. His name was Michael Winters, and his wife was called Bridget. I got Doris to meet them.

The next day, I was talking to Michael again and he asked me if I had ever been to Ireland. I had never been, but felt sure we would go there one day on holiday. He said he had a brother, Noel, who lived at the other end of Bentswood Road and they were going home in two weeks' time, and I would be welcome to go with them. Their parents lived in Strabane near Sion Mills. After a chat with Doris, I agreed to go. It was only from the Friday afternoon until the Sunday evening. We would fly from Gatwick to Belfast by Caledonian and the fare was £19 return. We would be picked up by another brother at Belfast and then a car journey of 85 miles. We arrived late that evening and met Mr and Mrs Winters, who had quite a large bungalow. Michael and Noel had not been back for some time, so all the neighbours came in and the celebrations went on until early morning. During my life, wherever I had been, I had never experienced such hospitality as I did that night and throughout the weekend. There was a very large family of Winters, 15 with the parents. On Saturday, as many of the brothers and sisters lived in that area, we spent visiting. In the evening it was arranged that we would be going to a hotel for an evening meal.

Strabane is situated just on the border between the north and south on the northern side. The hotel we were going to was over the border on the south side. It was called The Jackson. We left the bungalow that evening and passed over the border. I noticed that on each side of the border there were customs posts. We arrived at The Jackson and there were other relatives and friends waiting for us, in fact, there were 23 of us. Someone said the restaurant was full, and Michael asked for the manager, who welcomed us all in and gave us the private function room. A long table was laid while we were having drinks in the bar and I was being introduced to relatives and friends who had joined us. When we went into the function room, the manager had put some bottles of wine on the table with his compliments. We all had a very enjoyable evening, and it was late when we came out. I thought we would be going home. Michael and Noel asked me if I had ever been to a singing lounge. I had not, but would like to go. We all went into pub called the Galleon. There was a chap playing a piano accordion who was also a very good singer, and his name was Bill Quinn. In later years, I got to know him very well.

It was a fantastic weekend, and when we got home I told Doris that Mr and Mrs Winters were expecting us over, as they were looking forward to meeting Doris. The trouble was that Doris was frightened of flying. When at last Doris thought she would fly, we booked a holiday in Guernsey for one week. The plane we flew over on was a twin-propeller type and there were only about eight or so passengers. We also had the children with us. The captain came out during the flight and sat for a while with us, and he could see Doris was very nervous and he invited her into the cockpit. This was the best thing that could have happened. After this, Doris always looked forward to flying.

During our stay at a guest house in Guernsey, Doris suggested that we fly over to Jersey for a day, and this we did. We took a turn round the island. The beach was handy for the children. It was a very good holiday.

Raymond had not long left school, and we were working in Haywards Road when I was taken ill with back trouble. I was in Haywards Heath Cottage Hospital for a month on traction. I was in a bed being stretched out with weights on pulleys. I came home on crutches and was living on pain-killing tablets. This went on for six months. Ted Duffy had taken Raymond to work with him, and my work had more or less come to a close. Dr Dodd had now passed away and we had another, Dr Pritchard. He kept me supplied with pain tablets. I decided to go to the hospital at 9 o'clock on a Monday morning to see the consultant without an appointment. I was told the consultant I wanted to see was having to do two clinics as another consultant was ill. If I was to wait, they might be able to fit me in to see him, but not before between 12 and 1 o'clock. I said I would wait.

By 10 o'clock they had laid me flat on a table as I was in so much pain. They arranged for me to see the consultant straight away. I was in hospital and a disc was removed by the end of that week. I was embarrassed about my bleeding piles, as these were still very bad. Before the operation I asked the surgeon if he could avoid replacing the disc with a plastic one. I knew of two other people who had a plastic disc at that time and had never recovered to be able to work again. He could not assure me about that. That evening he came in to see me, and the first thing, I asked about the disc. He told me he had not replaced it, for which I was very thankful. The next morning they pulled me out of the bed and sat me in an armchair. I was screaming the ward down. They told me I would be in hospital about three weeks.

During my stay in hospital, Michael Winters never missed one evening to bring Doris over to see me and was always bringing me in cigarettes. Since my weekend in Ireland, we had become very good friends, and still are. Doris got on very well with Bridget, who was a great help with the children. Michael

143

and Bridget had been in rooms in Ashenground Road until they moved next door to us. They then had one girl called Patricia, and over the next few years they had two boys, Robert and Chris, and another girl called Mandy. All the children got on very well together. Doris and myself often said how lucky we were to have such good friends as neighbours.

I was told to learn to walk on my own again. This I did, and was discharged after ten days. Once I was home and recovering well, I was again faced with decision time as to whether I carried on on my own or found a job. I decided to carry on. I had a job to get my doctor to sign me off. I had to wait two months after the operation before he did. It was not many months before the work was going along very well. We decided to change the van to an estate car, which I changed for a Morris Oxford estate. This was more convenient to take the children in, and also we took it over to Ireland on the ferry from Liverpool.

There was another brother, Frank, who was just a bit younger than Michael, who was married and lived in the same road as the parents. They also made us very welcome. There were three younger brothers, Kevin, Robert and Brian, and one daughter, Bernadette, living with the parents the first time Doris and I stayed there. It never mattered how many of us there were, there was always accommodation. Whenever I was in Ireland, I always made a point to go out with a party of friends to hear Bill Quinn. Doris enjoyed his singing very much.

I was still very keen to learn to fly. Den Horton and myself joined a flying club at Biggin Hill. The lesson cost £6 an hour. It meant the loss of one day's work because of the journey and weather conditions changing. We took turns with the driving. We started our lessons in 1969. My instructor was a chap called Nick Ronayne. I was learning to fly Connor, Cherokee and Chipmunk, and Den was doing the same. We found it very helpful both of us doing the same thing, as we could compare our flying with each other. We were both hoping to get our private pilot's licence. I also became very friendly with a chap who maintained the aircraft for the club.

Den became ill, so I was going up on my own. There was a

Tiger Moth in the club and, although it was dual-controlled, it was not used for training purposes, only for private hire. I was having lunch with the maintenance man, whose name was Frank, when he asked me if I would like to go up in the Tiger Moth with him. That afternoon we went up, and I was able to take over the controls for a while. He took the controls back and asked me if I would like to do a loop and other aerobatics. That afternoon was a highlight of my flying. Frank told me later that he was with an aerobatics team at Biggin Hill.

I went up, one day, for a lesson, and Mick was not well and so an ex-Spitfire pilot was to take me up in an open two-seater Chipmunk. It was a clear day but very cold. He asked if I had some warmer clothes but as I had not, he let me have one of his ex-RAF flying suits, which he had used during the war. He explained to me that the intercom had not been working, but he had fixed it up with a dry battery which was fixed on the side of the front cockpit in which I would be sitting. He would be in the cockpit behind me. The lesson was to practice diving and pulling out. I carried out the usual checks, the intercom was working fine. At that stage of my flying I was taking off and landing. We took off, and I climbed to the height which Frank told me to. I straightened out, and he told me to dive. I was waiting for Frank to tell me to pull out when I realised something was wrong, and we were very low when Frank pulled us out of the dive. Frank's battery had become disconnected and fallen on the floor of the cockpit. We went over the river Thames for the next hour and had a good laugh when we got back. Frank insisted he would like me to have the flying suit as a present, so I put a donation into the club box. I used the suit many times.

It was in 1970–71 that there was trouble in the Middle East and the Suez Canal closed. As no ships could pass that way, they had to go all the way round South Africa and, as most of our fuel came from the Middle East, this put the price up in England very considerably. The price for flying lessons doubled to £12. This was too much so I had to give it up.

The family were now grown up. Valerie was 23 and nursing at the Royal Marsden in Sutton; Raymond was 22 and was now a partner in the business; Dennis, who, when he left school at 14, had gone into the Navy, had signed on for 12 years, and so had done about half of his time, and Richard had just left school and had come to work in the business. We now employed two fully qualified men and one apprentice. The business seemed to be growing very fast.

We were going over to Ireland about three times a year. We had toured around the south of Ireland and had been to Cork and met Bridget's mother and relations. They had a large farm outside Cork. It was about this time that Michael and Bridget decided to go back to Ireland to live. This, in a way, was a sad blow to Doris and myself, although we knew we would still be seeing them quite often. They had a firm of furniture removals come over from Strabane and they would load the van one day, stay the night and leave the next day. That evening we invited them in with the removal chaps and gave them all a farewell party.

After settling down back in Ireland, Michael and Bridget became members of the All Stars Club situated in Main Street, Strabane. The owner, Sean McGoldrick, his son, Seamus and manager, Charlie McBride, have always made us very welcome. Having got to know many of the members, we have spent many enjoyable evenings in this club.

Doris and myself decided we would go for a holiday on our own to America later that year, 1971. We spent our Silver Wedding anniversary, 8 June, in Ireland at a hotel over the border on the south side. We had a room for all our guests, and Bill Quinn played that evening. I had talked to Bill several times about coming to Haywards Heath. He had been over to Luton and Birmingham to the Irish clubs and Doris and myself had been to both places and stayed the weekend. Bill was very reluctant about coming south of London, as he thought there were no Irish clubs and his kind of music would not go very well. The first time Bill came to Luton he wrote to me to tell me the name of the club he would be playing at. One Saturday evening, Doris and I motored up to Luton and booked into a guest house. I asked the landlady, who was Irish, where the club was, and she said not too far away. She asked why we were

146

going to this club, and decided to come along herself after I had told her it was an Irish singer from Raphoe in Donegal. This was very handy, as she would drive us to the club.

Bill had assured me in his letter that we would all be able to get in, but when we arrived, the chap on the door told me it was strictly for members only. I asked if Bill had arrived, and he told me Bill was singing in Birmingham earlier that evening and was motoring down and was expected to arrive at any time. I asked if we could wait and this he agreed to, but not in the club. While we were waiting, I told him we had come up from Haywards Heath especially to hear Bill. He asked me what road we lived in, and I told him. He said his sister lived at no. 119 – it was Bridget's brother, Danny! I had heard her talk about Danny, but had not met him until now. We were then duly signed into the club. Bill was again playing to a packed audience. During the evening, Danny told me that when Bill had finished playing, and the bar had closed, to wait as there was going to be a private party for Bill and the bar would re-open! The next day we went to the club at lunchtime to say our farewells, as Doris and I were leaving to go back home.

Bill was a nurse at a hospital in Letterkenny in Donegal, married with a family of seven. He had a very nice bungalow on a hill looking over Raphoe, and the view looked out over the mountains of Donegal. He was very devoted to his work as a psychiatric nurse. One day we went to visit his home. His wife, Betty, made us very welcome. Bill took us into the Letterkenny hospital to meet the patients on his ward. They called Bill 'Dad'. They were so pleased to see him, and one could tell why he was devoted to looking after them. He also cut their hair; in fact he was a father and mother to them. Sometimes they would turn very violent because of their illness. Bill was a very tall, well built man and he told me that when a patient became violent it would take two or three nurses to calm him down. Bill had had the top of one of his fingers bitten off during one of the struggles. This was inconvenient when it happened, as Bill played a Transichord piano accordion. Bill always had a guitarist to play with him and also took on a drummer, whose name was Mike O'Hanlon. Mike had been a

147

professional, leading Ireland's first showband, The Clipper Carltons from 1951 to 1968, but had become the owner of a stationery shop in Strabane. The first time I heard Mike playing with Bill it was unbelievable, the talent Mike had. I was now trying more than ever to have them over to Haywards Heath.

Doris and myself left for our trip to America. We were invited to stay for a couple of days in Philadelphia by an Irish couple who had emigrated from Strabane many years before. We had never met them. We arrived in New York and took a limousine down to a hotel just outside Philadelphia, where our hostess met us and took us by car to her home. When we arrived at the house, Sadie, whose husband's name was Jerry, made us very welcome. We stayed for two days and left Philadelphia by Greyhound bus. We had bought a 14-day travel ticket to go wherever we wished in America or Canada. We planned where we would go and how long we would stay in certain places doing local tours. We returned to New York and then went to Niagara Falls then down the east coast to Orlando and Miami returning to Philadelphia, then on to Nashville as both of us enjoyed our country and western music. We returned home after three weeks and both of us thought this would be the holiday of our lifetime, never realising we would be going a few more times.

I had to go for a check-up after one year regarding my back, which was very good after having the disc removed. It was very sad to hear that the surgeon who had carried out my operation had been killed in a car crash while on holiday with his family in Germany. I told the consultant that since I had had the disc removed, the bleeding piles, which I had been suffering from since the war, had completely disappeared. After looking through my notes, he felt quite sure the disc had been displaced when I was blown out of the tank and had been touching a nerve, which had caused the piles. I am now 81, and have never had any trouble with anything like that since.

I had been telling Bill about St Francis Hospital, which was a very similar hospital to the one he worked in at Letterkenny. Also a large majority of the staff were Irish, and I had found out that they had a very nice club and a large hall called the Norman

148

Hay Hall. I also, at that time, used to go for a drink at a pub called the Ugly Duckling and I knew the landlord, Bill and his wife, Ivy, very well. On the first floor was a function room which Bill used to hire out. I spoke to Bill, the landlord, one evening about the singer I would like to get over from Ireland. He said that as I thought I could get about 60 people to come along (that is about all the room would hold), he would have someone on the bar and would not charge me for the hire of the room. I decided that, if I could get Bill to come, I would make it a private party and pay Bill myself plus his travelling expenses.

Armed now with how I could approach Bill, we went over to Ireland. During our stay we went over to visit Betty and Bill and while there, I asked him if we could have a private chat. While Doris stayed with Betty, we went into Raphoe to a pub for a drink. While we were there, Bill was telling me how his father used to own the pub called Frields. I put my proposition to Bill and he told me that, if he agreed, could I find them somewhere to stay. I told him they would be staying with us. After I had been trying for five years, Bill said he would come. I left it to him when he could manage a weekend, as he was booked up far ahead on Saturday evenings. Before we came home he had given me a date. I had phoned the landlord of the Ugly Duckling to make sure that the room was vacant. All I had to do was to find 60 people to come along and we would discover whether Bill was right about his kind of music south of London.

I had no bother finding support for the party, particularly when it was free. I asked Ivy if she would supply nibbles for the tables and sandwiches for the break. When the evening arrived, about half an hour before they were due to come on, Mike was a nervous wreck. This surprised me, as he had been in the entertainment business all his life. He told me it was always the same, each time he was due to go on. The evening was more than a great success. During the interval I had to go down into the lounge bar. I spoke to a chap called Peter Elmer, of a very large and powerful build. Now Peter was a chap who loved music on a Saturday evening, and when the bars were full, Peter would always start the singing. It would end with everyone in all the bars singing, with Peter louder than everyone else. Peter

149

asked me who had been singing upstairs. I told him, and he said he and his friend were coming up. I do not know how it was that I had not invited him, but I explained we were full up with no more room. He started to take his jacket off and asked me if I was going to stop him. I told him to go up! Peter and his friend were so taken with Bill and Mike he asked me if I would mind if he could make a collection for them. I explained that they had already been paid and it was not necessary, but again, he asked if I was going to stop him. He collected £100, which was then a good sum of money. The strange thing was, I had not invited any Irish from the hospital, as I did not, at that time, know any of them there.

My sister had died quite young with cancer, and her husband, Fred, had moved into a flat in Cuckfield. He had sold the house to his youngest daughter, Janet, who was married to an Irish chap called Paddy Hyde. They were very good neighbours. Noel Winters, who I first went over to Ireland with, had now moved back to Ireland. Michael and Bridget now had a three-bedroomed house at the Glebe, Sion Mills. This was about three miles from Michael's parents. Noel was also living at the Glebe. We were going over at least twice a year. Mr Winters passed away and I was not well enough, at that time, to go over for the wake and funeral. Mrs Winters rented the bungalow from the Council, and Michael decided to buy the bungalow for the future. His mother still stayed in the bungalow. It was about this time that the troubles started in the north. Doris and myself were in Londonderry the first day, which was a Sunday, when the fighting broke out in Derry. As the troubles became worse, Strabane became a flashpoint, being on the border. It became so bad that it would not be safe to take my car any more. In Strabane a car with English number plates would have been burnt. I opened an account with Avis car hire, and I would phone them and they would have a car waiting at Aldergrove airport when we arrived.

Doris and myself went over several times. During one of our visits, Michael's son, Robert, was going out deep-sea fishing off the coast of Donegal, and he invited me along on one of his trips. There were 17 of us, and I was given a rod to try my hand.

150

I managed to bring a few up, more by luck than judgement. It was the first time in my life I had held a rod. Pat Robinson, the skipper, invited me into his cabin. From here he controlled the boat, called the *Cricket*, and the radar, which showed shoals of fish under the boat. We went about 40 miles out in the Atlantic. We came back in the evening to the little port of Port-Na-Blagh, and on the way home we stopped at a pub for drinks and an evening meal. It was an incredible day out. The next time it was shark fishing. There were four rods on the side of the boat with lines away out. Each line had a coloured ball on over the hook. The bait had been laid for the sharks. Normal fishing took place during the day, and it was during the afternoon that a shout went up and a bell was ringing that a shark had taken the hook. It was Michael's rod, so he took over pulling it in. Pat put a strap around Michael, which was connected to the rod. The shark was very soon brought into the boat and weighed in at 35 lbs. It was then returned back into the sea to swim away. Soon after this the second one got hooked, and this rod was Michael's son, Chris. When his was weighed it was 85 lbs. Another very good day out. I look forward to going out many more times yet. Robert is now the organiser of parties going out on the *Cricket*.

Doris and I had a bad experience on a Sunday. At that time no bars or lounges were allowed to open on Sundays in the north. We would go over the border to the south, where the bars were open, for a lunchtime drink. Doris and I left the bungalow about 11.45 to go over to the Glebe to pick up Michael and Noel. There was a pub about a mile from the bungalow called the Mourne Bar. I knew this pub very well and John, the landlord, his wife and small family. As we were just about to pass the pub, John ran across the road in front of my car to a pair of cottages opposite. As we passed, I saw a car parked in front of the pub, and I remarked to Doris that it appeared that the pub might be open. We had just passed when there was an explosion. It lifted our car up and back down on the road. The car in front of the pub had exploded, blowing most of the front of the pub out. John told me later he had received a phone call and had got his wife and children out the back along by the Mourne river. He had run across to warn the people in the cottages. No one was injured, and on the Monday I went down to see John. He had a notice at the front, business as usual – round the back. John had received a letter on the previous Thursday, as had all the other bars, not to open. John had ignored it and opened as usual, and this was the penalty. It was later rebuilt with vast improvements.

Paddy Hyde and Janet had two boys. Paddy and the boys played table tennis at St Francis club, and I asked him if he could arrange for me to have a meeting with someone on the entertainments committee at the club. This he did, and Paddy came up with me to introduce me to Frank Dolon, who was chairman. I took some posters of Bill and Mike, but Frank was very reluctant to book them. He said he was responsible for booking groups and had never booked a group and lost money. Also, he did not feel they could cover the whole evening and he would also have to book a disco. I knew the fee Bill and Mike would expect. After two hours, I was about to give up with him when I asked, if he did book them, how much would the entrance tickets be. He told me £1. I then asked him that, if I could bring guests, how many of us would be allowed in. He told me as many as I liked and we could be signed in on a block booking. That was fine, I said, let me have 50 tickets and I may even want more. I said that they would only play on their own and no disco. At last he agreed, and it was only left now to find out the dates when Bill would be free to come. This was soon arranged, and I had no trouble selling my first 50 tickets.

Bill and Mike now had a short musical cabaret, which they performed midway during the show. Mike could impersonate many artists, such as Mohammed Ali, Groucho Marx, Frank Carson and many others, and Bill's impersonation was of Jim Reeves. He had recorded two albums which had sold more than one million copies. During the evening, word had gone round about this singer from Ireland, and several offered to pay £5 to come in for the rest of the evening. They made a terrific impact on the club that evening, and Frank invited us up to the club on the Sunday lunchtime. He was very keen to book them the next time, not only in the club but in the Norman Hay Hall, which could hold 300 to 350. Bill could not believe the reception they

152

were getting and said they would be looking forward to coming again.

I managed, through friends and relatives, to book other halls in Mid-Sussex. Bill, Mike, and Bill's nephew, Gill Quinn, came over for several years for sometimes one, two or three weeks, whenever Bill had his holiday from the hospital. They always stayed with us, and I had to have someone to give Doris a hand with the meals. We enjoyed every moment. Mike was a great character to have around the house. He loved to play jokes on people. One morning, we were all going up to the town shopping when the doorbell rang. I answered, and a man with a beard and flat cap said the taxi we had ordered was waiting. I had quite a job to convince him – it was Mike. I never dreamed it was him. He could really play the part.

They came over for three weeks, and during that time they only had one night each week when they were not playing. One of these evenings we decided to go to the Ringmer Hotel for a meal. At that time the Ringmer was putting on some very good cabarets with well known artists. Doris's sister Kathleen, although she enjoyed coming out, I think she would agree that Irish singing was not really her cup of tea. After the meal, the cabaret started. It was a very well known singer with his own band. During the cabaret he asked for a singer to join him on stage to do a duet. No one would go up, so he came across to our table and pulled Kath out of her seat and onto the stage. We could see how embarrassed she was, in fact, she was almost in tears. I asked Bill to go and get her out of trouble. Although Bill had met Kath only once before, he knew she was very shy.

Bill then went onto the stage, took the microphone out of Kath's hand and carried on the singing. The artist stopped singing and let Bill carry on on his own. When the number was finished, Bill came back to our table, but the audience insisted that he went on stage for one more number. Bill was on stage for half an hour. I noticed that while he was singing, the waiters, waitresses, chefs, in fact all the staff, including the manager, were standing in, listening to Bill. The manager came to our table and wanted to book Bill, who said that he was not a

153

professional. The manager could not believe this. However, he sent a bottle of best wine to our table.

The last Saturday evening of that three weeks was in the Norman Hay Hall as usual, completely packed out. Many of the audience never missed one evening whenever Bill was playing. I had often asked for a *Mid-Sussex Times* reporter to come along, and I was very pleased that evening when Rick Peckham introduced himself as the reporter. During the breaks he was with Bill and Mike. He wrote an excellent report in the *Mid-Sussex Times*, for 4 December 1975, and here are a few comments from that report. It was headed 'The Man Who Captivates All Ages'. 'With so much professional quality and composure it is hard to believe that Bill is only a part-time musician who fills most of his days with his duties as a psychiatric nurse in Donegal. His two Jim Reeves albums have sold more than million copies and another stroke of luck that local tradesman Fred Goddard saw him playing in Ireland and eventually managed to persuade him to play over here. His first concert in Haywards Heath was two and half years ago and since has built a large Mid-Sussex following. Nutty Mike from Strabane is the only one with a professional background, leading Ireland's first show band the "Clipper Carltons". When Rick asked Bill if he played in Ulster he answered, "Not since the tragic murder of the Miami Showband." Bill's popularity in Mid-Sussex is obvious but it took Fred Goddard a long time to persuade him to make the first trip. "I thought he was putting me on and that we would be wasting our time," said Bill.'

Doris and myself enjoyed every moment we had them over, and I would like to say now that we never took any money for their keep or from the money they earned. In fact, it cost me money being out so much, Doris thought I was becoming an alcoholic. Bill liked a drink, but not when he was playing. He would enjoy one when he was finished. Mike had never drunk or smoked during his lifetime.

I received a letter one day from a lady called Hilda. She was a nanny to a Jewish boy in London. Hilda was born in Sligo, Ireland, and while on holiday in Sligo, Bill and Mike had been playing in a hotel and she had been taken up with Bill's singing

154

of the Jim Reeves numbers. Because of the write-up in the *Mid-Sussex Times* she had tracked down my address, to ask if she could come when Bill was here singing. When Bill came the next time, I contacted her. The boy she had been nanny to was now about to get married and she asked that, as he and his future wife would drive her down, whether I would reserve three places for them. Doris said why not invite them down early and we could all have tea together. I now had Hilda's phone number. She lived in a flat in Warwick Gardens, Kensington. I phoned, and she was so pleased to be able to come down early. They arrived and we were introduced to Roberta and Derek. Bill remembered Hilda from Sligo. Roberta and Derek spent most of the time with our radiogram, playing records. Hilda was telling us she had brought Derek up from a baby. His parents, who were very wealthy, owned the largest furriers in Oxford Street. They came to every show when Bill was playing. They never stayed overnight, but sometimes spent most of the afternoon with us.

Doris and I were very surprised when we received an invitation to the wedding, which was at a synagogue in Bayswater, with a reception at the Herbert Samuel Hall. This was to be a new experience for us, not having ever been in a synagogue before or to a Jewish wedding. It was quite a relief when we heard Bill and Mike would be playing at the reception. Bill, Mike, Doris and myself had been booked into a hotel in Bayswater the day before the wedding. In the synagogue all the women sat over one side and the men at the other. As I seemed to be lost as to what was happening, the men each side explained everything as we went along with the ceremony.

When we arrived at the hall, one room was laid out with all kinds of drinks. Here we met and everyone was introducing themselves. It was a very friendly atmosphere, unlike our weddings, where the two sides are kept apart and only get to know each other at the end of the day. After this we moved into another hall for the meal. Up to now, we had not seen Bill or Mike since leaving the hotel. After the meal, we moved into another hall and here we were introduced by the Toastmaster, and as he called out 'Mr and Mrs F. Goddard', there was a roll on the drums, you can guess who it was – Bill, Mike and Gill, ready to play. They were dressed in new outfits and the stage was a mass of flowers. I was told that the outfits and flowers cost £1,500. There was a bar and food. I was surprised how much food was consumed that day. It was not all consumed by the guests. As it was a very warm day, most of the windows were open. There were lots of children outside, obviously from the poorer areas around there, scrounging for food. I managed to pass quite a lot through the windows to the kids. Doris got very worried when I started to do this, but it was not long before I noticed Doris doing the same thing. I feel sure there were not many at that reception who had ever known what it was like to be hungry. At midnight, the climax to the day was when the waitresses came in with silver trays piled up with hot doughnuts. It was a day to be remembered. The next day the four of us carried out a tour of London and then went home.

The business was going very well. Richard had now passed his college training in plumbing and held a City and Guilds Advanced Certificate, the same as Raymond. We took another apprentice, Stutley Upton. Stutley was the brother of Heather, whose father, with several of his brothers, owned a large furniture shop on the Broadway, Haywards Heath. Raymond and Heather had been courting a few years before then, but had drifted apart.

All the apprentices we had taken on went to college, and all gained their City and Guilds Advanced Certificates. Richard was a great help in the business, and I felt sure it would not be long before he would be a partner.

Doris and I decided to go to America for another holiday, now that we knew Frank Dolan and his wife very well. Frank also had a sister who lived just outside New York. When Frank knew that we were going, he arranged with his sister for us to stay with her and her husband for three days. We flew into New York, met them and they took us out to their home, about six miles out of New York. We had a very nice basement apartment. Frank's brother-in-law, Tom, had a very high position with the social security in New York, so each morning he would drive us in, making a list of places to visit all written out in detail. This went very well, and we would meet him later that day to go back home. We were very grateful for those three days as we learnt so much about New York from Tom. We then flew across America to San Francisco. We only intended to stay for one day, so we took a tour in a limousine with another couple. We drove around the whole of San Francisco. There was so much to see, we felt we must stay a few days. In the afternoon we visited a lovely cathedral called St Mary's. The next morning we took a tour of the redwoods, and in the afternoon we paid a visit to the fisherman's wharf and were so taken up with the entertainment down on the wharf that we stayed for three days. The tram rides were something not to be missed. We were down on the wharf when we saw there were helicopter flights over the bridge and harbour. These rides lasted about ten minutes. There was a queue at the box office, and when I asked for two tickets I was told it was my lucky day as on our trip we would be going to another airfield to pick up another pilot. The trip would take about 30 minutes.

We flew out over San Francisco, picked up the pilot and coming back he was pointing out to us many things about the city. He also asked the pilot of the helicopter to go over Alcatraz Prison and the San Francisco bridge. The trip lasted for 45 minutes. We would have liked to stay in San Francisco longer, but had to move on. We again travelled with Greyhound across America to Reno, where we visited the casinos in the evening and then travelled all night to Salt Lake City. We went up in the Rockies in an old steam train with open-seater trucks and then, taking in many local tours at each main town, on to Cheyenne, Denver, Colorado Springs, Kansas City, St. Louis, Nashville (Opry land), and then one whole day in Philadelphia, then New York and home.

When we arrived back, there was a letter from Bill to explain that he would be playing again in Haywards Heath but someone else would be making the arrangements and bookings. I had suspected this might happen, as I knew the chap who had stated he would like to take Bill over. It did not worry me very much because I felt it was a lot of work for Doris, and also I knew it would not last.

157

We were in Ireland quite often and could go and hear Bill anytime. I heard the first time Bill came they were staying in a guest house in Haywards Heath and were only playing for two evenings. One was in the club at St Francis, and one of my sons was there that evening and told me when the evening had finished there was a terrific row over money between Frank Dolan, Bill and the chap who had brought Bill over. That was the last time Bill played in Haywards Heath.

Our son Dennis, who was in the Navy and stationed at Portsmouth, came home on leave between sea trips. He phoned to say he had a leave but would not be coming home this time. One of his mates was being married in Hull, and Dennis was going to be the best man. A few months after this he phoned to say that when he was at his mate's wedding he had met a girl and was going to be engaged. He also said, after a while on the phone, that she had a small baby, but sounded very relieved when we said how pleased we were. It was arranged that he bring Sylvia down and we would give them an engagement party at the Ugly Duckling. Her parents would look after the baby. This went very well, and Dennis had some of his old friends at the party. Ivy laid on a very good buffet. Doris and myself thought Sylvia a very nice, hard-working girl. The wedding was arranged to be on 11 January 1978 at Sylvia's church near her home. It was a very quiet wedding with a reception at Sylvia's home in the afternoon, followed by a get-together in the local hotel. After a very nice wedding and weekend, Dennis, Sylvia and the baby left for Portsmouth, where they had been allotted a Navy flat. It was very sad for Sylvia's parents, as they had become very attached to the baby, because they had looked after it most of the time while Sylvia was at work as a hairdresser.

I became involved in another incident in about 1978. I went over to Ireland for a week on my own. The troubles were still very much alive, although the week I had stayed there had been very quiet. I was due to fly back on a Monday evening and was in Strabane on the Monday morning when I was talking to Bill. He told me he was giving a concert in the Inter County Hotel, which was in Lifford just over the border bridge. I told Bill if

158

everything was alright at home I might stay over until the following Thursday and come over to the hotel on the Wednesday evening for the concert. I phoned Doris and as all was well, had my return ticket altered. I had a car from Avis on hire and altered the hire period to the Thursday. On the Wednesday evening I left with a full car. Noel followed behind in his car, and altogether there were ten of us.

We went through Strabane and came to the bridge. I thought it very unusual that there were no lights. There was an Army checkpoint and an officer came over to me and asked me to put the lights out on my car, and he then said he thought it was OK to go across but not to put the lights on and to cross slowly. I started to move away very slowly until Noel had come through the checkpoint, when he was behind me we moved slowly across. I came to the middle on the bridge and I saw flashes from a building on the south side of the bridge and realised we were being fired at from that side. I also realised I could not do a three-point turn on the centre of the bridge to go back as Noel was behind me, and also I would have put the passengers at more risk with the car being sideways on. I decided the only thing to do was to put my headlights on full and my foot down hard on the accelerator. The hotel was only about 200 yards after leaving the bridge. We went into the hotel and most of us called for a large whiskey. Bill never mentioned about the other chap who took over from me, and I never mentioned it to him. I believe it was very embarrassing for him.

14

Retirement

In 1981 I retired from full-time working. Our daughter, Valerie, attended the Evangelist Church in New England Road, and it was here she met Gordon Upton, a son of Steve, another of the Upton brothers from the furniture business. Valerie and Gordon had become engaged while we were away on our last trip to America. This was a very big shock to Doris and me, as Valerie was so devoted to her nursing and had never bothered about boyfriends. However, we felt they were very suited to each other. The wedding was planned for 2 May 1981, and was held at their church, followed by a reception in the hall behind the church. Dennis and his family came up from Portsmouth. The happy couple started married life in a terraced cottage in Burgess Hill and carried out modernisations.

The business was going along very successfully. Richard was now a partner with Raymond, and they employed several men, all fully qualified. In Lindfield was an old-established plumbing firm by the name of Ede's. It was founded soon after the war and was taken over on Mr Ede's retirement by his employee, Roy Mitchell, in about 1960. Roy employed a chap called Ted Gower, and Ted had never driven or held a driving licence. Roy and Ted worked very well together for 20 years. I knew Roy fairly well, and one day I was talking to him, and he told me he was not keeping in the best of health. He was coming up to retirement himself and was looking for another firm to take over his business. The premises Roy leased were behind the Post Office and there was a workshop and an office and

160

stores. Roy told me there were two large firms interested in taking over and he was on the verge of making a choice. I, myself, was about to retire, and Roy asked me if I thought my sons would be interested, as he would rather our family business take it over than either of the larger firms. Also, if one of these firms took over, it must affect our business. Roy was also worried about Ted as he was about 58 years old. I told Roy I would talk to my sons at lunchtime that day and assured him they would phone him soon after lunch the same day. They did phone to arrange a meeting. They had decided to take over from Roy and employ Ted. At that time we employed four fully qualified plumbers and electricians. After Ted had been with us a few months, during which time he had taken driving lessons and had passed his test first time, we had a very good write up by the *Mid-Sussex Times*, with pictures of our employees.

I put in a few hours during the mornings doing office work, and it was not long before we employed a secretary, and when she was capable I became a 'sleeping' partner. It was not long before I was restless and looking for something different to do.

We were talking one evening about what I could do, and I cannot remember if it was Raymond or Richard who suggested why not take up wine making, and this I decided to do as I had no idea about wines. Whenever I was at a wedding reception, which was the only time I drank wine, other people there would be commenting about the wine being very dry or sweet or perhaps medium dry or sweet, and I had no idea what they were talking about. I just drank it, and to me it was just wine. I saw an advertisement that at our local college was a beginners wine course starting during the winter evenings at Harlands College. I enrolled to go on this. When the course was completed I knew how to make wines, but at the same time realised there was more to learn by experience. There was a shop in Haywards Heath called the Healthy Brewer, and this shop supplied everything for making home-made wines. It was owned by a chap named Lawrie Stevens who I had become friendly with, as I was buying quite a lot of equipment used in home wine and beer making. Lawrie was very helpful when I had a problem, but suggested it would help me a lot if I joined the Haywards

161

Heath Wine and Beer Guild. I did not fancy doing this, as I thought they would all be experts and I was only a learner, but Lawrie convinced me this was not so and suggested I went and sat in one evening and to decide after if I wanted to join or not.

The club held their meetings once a month at the King Edward Hall in Lindfield. I went along and sat at a table on my own. They were all drinking each other's wines; I found out later it was called a wine whist evening, but I had not taken any wine with me. When the meeting ended a lady came over and asked me if I was interested in joining, but I was very undecided after sitting on my own for two hours and told her I would perhaps join the next time. I went to the next meeting, and this time I was made very welcome. Also this time my hairdresser, Vic Hayden, who I know quite well, and his wife, Edna, who had hardly missed a Bill Quinn evening, were there. I joined the club and everyone was very helpful. I was now making wine five gallons at a time and enjoyed making country wines. The club belonged to the Sussex Federation who annually held a wine competition at Clair Hall, Haywards Heath. This involved many wine clubs in Mid-Sussex. Usually there would be about 1,000 bottles of home-made wine entered in their different classes.

The first time I entered some of my wines I was not expecting any of them to be given any place in the judging, but was more interested in the criticism by the judges. The wines had to be entered early in the morning. No one was allowed in the hall while the judging was carried out up to lunchtime. During the afternoon we could then go into the hall and they had what they called 'Judges at the Bar'. This meant the judges would stand by their own class of wines which they had judged and would give the entrant their opinion and criticism of an entrant's particular wine. The first judge I asked about a dry wine I had entered looked down his list for my number, and looking at me, he remarked, 'This bottle I have put down as water!' This rather upset me, as I had been looking forward to his comments. He then remarked that it was unfortunate that I had entered it in the wrong class, as it was a sweet wine. When I checked with the other wine I had entered in the sweet class it was in fact a dry wine and I had got my entries crossed over. I made sure that would not happen again. I settled down with the club very well and became their treasurer for nine years. I still belong to the club, although very few members these days make home made wine.

It was 8 June 1986, when Doris and I celebrated our Ruby wedding anniversary. We held this in a function room in a pub called the Pilgrim. This pub is just around the corner from our house, and the landlord and landlady, who Doris and myself knew very well as Ray and Barbara Gardner, engaged musicians. One of our favourite artists around, at that time, were a married couple called Yvonne and Norman, The Champions, and through Ray we were able to book them for the evening. The function room was on the ground floor with its own bar, stage and dance floor opening out on to a very nice lawn. Ray arranged that we had our own barman, by the name of Terry Gasson. Terry really helped to make our evening as he was a very jovial person and created many laughs at the bar. Bridget, Michael, Noel, Jennifer, Frank and Teresa all came over from Ireland. Bridget had a sister who lived in Three Bridges and we invited them, but it was kept a secret from Bridget that her sister would be there. Most of the members of the wine club came along, and Ray allowed them to bring their home-made wine in with them. Altogether there were 135 guests that evening.

I was still a very heavy smoker, so it was not surprising when I had my first heart attack. Dr Pritchard had retired and my present doctor, Dr Harding, was called in. I was in Cuckfield Hospital for two weeks. Just before being discharged, several chaps who had also had heart attacks were given a lecture on drinking and smoking. None of us had been allowed to smoke while in that ward for two weeks. The sister remarked that when we came back for our check-ups we would all be smoking again. I felt the time had come to give up, but it would not be easy, as I had been smoking 80 to 100 a day. I can only class the next six weeks as hell. I went to my doctor to see if he could help as I did not want to start again, and he gave me a tonic. I did not think it would help, but after taking it for about a week the craving started to wear off. I found I was perhaps taking more than was prescribed. As Doris had to go to Dr Harding, she asked him if I could have some more tonic. He prescribed another bottle, but told Doris he would not be giving me any more. I realised that, although the craving to smoke was much easier, I was perhaps getting hooked on the tonic. It took a few years to lose the craving.

Our son, Richard, met a girl from Henfield by the name of Gillian Sutton. They had been courting for quite a while when we were invited to Henfield to meet her parents. We all got on very well together, and it was not long before Richard announced they were getting married on 29 August 1987. They would be getting married at Henfield church, with a reception at the Pilgrim Hotel. Gillian's parents, Eileen and Michael, had not been to the Pilgrim before, so we invited them along one evening to see the function room which we had for our Ruby anniversary. They agreed it was ideal for the reception. In our business, we use a firm to service our vehicles called DPC, which is owned by a chap called Dave Chewter. Dave had a few very old vintage cars which he hired out for special occasions. Richard hired an open seater for the wedding, which Dave drove himself. Dennis came up with the family and was best man and, as he was now a Petty Officer, he looked very smart in his uniform. It was a very good day. Ray and Barbara at the Pilgrim were very easy-going and helpful. Richard and Gillian left at the end for a honeymoon in Jersey.

I had another two heart attacks, but not as bad as the first. I was only in hospital for one week in each case.

In 1987 I achieved two diplomas at Clair Hall in the Sussex Federation of Wine Makers competition, one First Class and one Very Highly Commended; in 1988, one Highly Commended; 1989, one First and a Second; 1990, one Highly Commended; 1991, three Thirds, and, in the Horticultural Society shows, two Firsts, five Seconds and four Thirds.

My son Raymond had a very good friend, Paddy Henry. Paddy had also become a friend of the family, coming into the house whenever he wished and enjoying not only cups of tea but the chats with Doris. Paddy had worked for the NHS, but because of a dispute he had taken the NHS to court and won the case. Paddy has not worked since, but is very involved in unions and he is also a Town and District Councillor with my son Richard. Paddy and Richard won Labour seats in 1991, the first time seats had gone to Labour for 17 years.

It was about this time that I became ill with diverticulitis. I was taken into Cuckfield Hospital, but deteriorated very fast. Paddy came to visit me one Sunday afternoon and seemed very concerned as to why they were not getting on with the operation. I told Paddy that they had told me it was diverticulitis but had not explained any details of what that was. He explained it all to me and even drew out a diagram of the bowel and stoppage and said that they had tried starving and now were left with only one answer, an operation, and he could not understand why they had not got on and done this. Now that I was armed with this information, I said I would be able to ask Mr Corbett why the delay. I could never understand why doctors and surgeons are so secretive in not explaining more details of the patient's complaint. When I was told I had diverticulitis I could not pronounce it or spell it, and certainly had not a clue to what it meant.

Mr Corbett, the surgeon, told me he could operate but was declining to do so because of my three heart attacks. He felt sure I would not survive a major operation. He said that if I was in a corner he would carry out the operation. A few days later I remember drifting away but could hear the nurses talking to me, saying I had a temperature and they were covering me with some wet blankets to get the temperature down. The next thing I remember, I was in the intensive care unit with a male nurse who kept waking me up to take my blood pressure. I asked him to leave me alone. I felt I had had enough. I do not know how long I was in the intensive care unit, but I recovered enough to go back to the ward.

During the next few days in the ward I could not get any sleep because of the pain. I watched it getting dark when they pulled the blinds down and watched it getting light in the mornings. I knew now the pain would soon be going, with each day, as I had been in this situation many times before. I had a bag on the front on my stomach which everything discharged into from the bowel, the smell was terrible. One patient two beds from mine discharged himself because he insisted on my being moved out of the ward, and this they refused to do. As I improved, I was given instructions so as to be able to change the bag myself. I was very pleased to be told that after about two to three months I could have another operation to reverse things back to normal and dispose of the bag. This would depend on the result of an X-ray. I had the X-ray, and Mr Corbett, because he knew how keen I was to get rid of this bag, phoned me to say the X-ray was OK and I could have the reverse operation. He asked when I would like it done, and I said the next day if possible. He then informed me that he was going on holiday the next day for two weeks, but would make arrangements for one of his colleagues to carry out the reversal. I declined this offer. I would rather wait until he returned from holiday. Doris was very good helping with the changing of the bag. I understand it is not always possible to have the reverse operation and many people have to live with a bag for the rest of their lives. I sympathise with them very much. Hopefully, this situation has improved in the time since I had my operation.

After the two weeks, and on the day I knew Mr Corbett had returned from his holiday, I received a phone call in the afternoon from him that, providing there was a bed, I could go in on the following Monday and have the operation on the Tuesday. This was carried out successfully, and I returned to normal life with many thanks to Mr Corbett.

Doris and myself decided we would like to have some kind of home work, so we investigated several jobs we could do. About this time we saw an advertisement for assembling micro switches. This was a firm called Otehall Switches, who had a factory in Burgess Hill but were about to move their factory to Wivelsfield Green. We went to Burgess Hill and got the parts and started our home work. We worked under a chap called Colin Lay for a few years and then on other types of switches. I gave up the switches to write this book, but if my health is still good when I have finished, I would like to start doing them again. We had been working for ten years doing the switches

166

and enjoyed doing them. Colin, the van driver, calls to see me from time to time. I am a great believer in keeping fingers moving to hold off arthritis.

I received a phone call one Monday morning that Mrs Winters had died. I went to Ireland that same afternoon for the wake and funeral. Bill came over as well, and later we went for a drink. He told me he had taken early retirement from the hospital and was working odd times for Radio Letterkenny as a DJ. He had always been involved with this station and almost every day they would play one of his recordings.

Now that I had made a full recovery from the diverticulitis, Doris and I decided to have another holiday in America. This time we flew into Los Angeles, and as usual we stayed for a few days there, exploring the city, and then set out on a new route back to New York. Our main highlight on this holiday was to see the Grand Canyon. We left Los Angeles on the Greyhound to Phoenix. We arrived late at night, and this was the only night that Doris and I could not get a bed and had to sleep in the bus station. After a good breakfast we hired a car with another couple and toured the Grand Canyon. We stopped at various places around the Canyon. Looking down at different angles into the Canyon it shows as the four seasons. It is a magnificent sight.

We then moved to El Paso, and here we became very good friends with a Mexican family who owned a bar and café. They gave us a very nice plate as a souvenir. We then went to Dallas, but did not stay as it was too hot. We carried on to St. Louis, New Orleans and of course Nashville, doing all that has to be done in these places and many other places we visited. We then travelled all one day and one night on the Greyhound to be in Philadelphia in the early morning to spend our last few days with Sadie and Jerry. Then on to New York and home.

Bridget's brother, Danny, who we met in Luton, had lived there most of his life, but on retiring, he married a very nice girl from Donegal. Although they were married in Luton, they held the reception in Donegal, to which Doris and I were invited. They had a bungalow built in Donegal and are now enjoying retired life. In southern Ireland, pensioners receive free travel

167

on public transport which I understand, now applies in Northern Ireland. They do not pay for a television licence and receive higher pensions.

During 1987, I started to get trouble with my head wound. From time to time it became very inflamed and my hairdresser, Vic, had had to be very careful when cutting my hair. It was also very painful. I went to see my doctor, who prescribed painkiller tablets which helped a lot.

We received an invitation to Sadie and Jerry's daughter Elaine's wedding, and so we decided to go to Philadelphia for one week. The wedding was very different in many ways to ours at home, which made it very enjoyable. Sadie and Jerry made us very welcome as usual.

It was in January 1992 that I received the sad news that Bill Quinn had passed away, aged 56. Just about this time I was not all that well with pains in my chest, so I could not travel to go over to Ireland for the funeral.

The pains became more severe, and in March I was admitted to hospital. A new hospital had recently been built in Haywards Heath, called the Princess Royal Hospital. I went into Balcombe Ward under Dr Metcalfe, who diagnosed my problem as angina. After a week I was discharged. I was admitted and discharged four times with the same problem from March to May. Each time I was admitted to Balcombe Ward, and the nurses would ask if I had brought my switches with me. Whenever I was able to sit in the day room, Doris would spend many hours with me there, assembling our switches. Other patients were quite envious of our pastime. The money we received from the switches was used for holidays.

During my last stay in Balcombe Ward I went up to Kings College in London for tests. From the results of these, I was told I needed a double heart bypass and a new valve in my heart. On my return to Balcombe Ward I was discharged almost immediately, to wait my turn for the operation. I came home on a Friday and by the Sunday had become much worse. Doris called in Dr Harding, who had me admitted that afternoon. On arriving back in Balcombe Ward a doctor examined me and I was taken straight away to the theatre to have a temporary pace-

168

maker fitted. I feel sure that as this was carried out so quickly it saved my life. As the machine had increased my heart rate, I felt much better. When Dr Metcalfe came on her rounds on the Monday morning I am afraid I blew my top as to why I had been delayed so long in having the operation. Dr Harding had also requested her to ring him that morning, which she did.

My daughter, Valerie, who was working now as a sister in the hospital, along with my sons Raymond and Richard insisted on seeing a doctor that Monday evening, to see what could be done if I was to go as a private patient. They had consulted Dr Harding about this. He was not in favour because it could cause a longer delay, as they would have to carry out tests which I had already had. I felt it was because I was now 75 and age was the reason, and of course my previous heart attacks. I had had to bang on the table at the POW camp, and I was banging it again now.

By the end of that week I was in Kings College to have the operation. The day before my operation I was asked if some students could carry out a cardiac examination on me because I had a particular heart murmur. This I agreed to, but was surprised I had been asked, and was told that not all patients would agree to this. The students came in batches of about eight at a time. In fact I found it quite interesting, as they were strictly told off if they omitted anything in the procedure of the examination. Some I felt sorry for. I do not know how many examinations I had that day, but only three students traced the heart murmur. The man who was in charge of all this came in to thank me. I said it was a pity I had not charged half a guinea a time, as I never realised there would be so many and that I now felt I could do a cardiac examination as well as the students. We had a good laugh, and he wished me luck for the next day and said he would drop in to see me after the operation.

During my stay in Kings, I became friendly with a chap by the name of Sidney Clarke. Sid owns the old picture shop in the famous Brighton Lanes. I found Sid very interesting to talk to and although we have spoken to each other on the phone since then, we have yet to meet again. Sid had a quadruple bypass and recovered well.

On the morning of the operation, I went down to have a wash and shave early. There was another chap having a wash, and he had been waiting several months to come in for a triple bypass. He was also having his done that day. I thought he was only about 30. When the papers came round I bought an *Express* to read while they were preparing me for the theatre. While reading the paper, my eye caught the word horoscope. This is something I would never bother to read, but because it was the day of my operation thought I would read it. It was dated 13 May 1992, Sagittarius, and it read, 'Your brain has non-functioning days when common sense seems to desert you. Be prepared to sit quietly until daylight dawns'.

For about three days before this, the physiotherapist had been teaching me exercises which she wanted me to do after the operation. I came round clutching a very large, very hard teddy bear, and I noticed several other chaps in beds opposite, also hugging teddy bears. I had been told that when the pain was very bad I should hug the bear very tightly to my chest and this would help to relieve the pain. It did work! The physiotherapist came to give me the exercises I had been taught. She told me she came into the intensive care unit to see me, and although I had not come round she spoke to me and as soon as I heard her voice I started to do the exercises. That's what I call being brainwashed! She got me out of bed within a few days and took me down the passage for a walk. I quickly became very tired and she let me have a rest. After a short rest I turned to go back to the ward, and she then said how would I feel about going up some stairs. I have never turned down a challenge and managed to walk up the first flight. I was very pleased to get back to the ward, but more than pleased with the walk. By the end of May, although I had not yet had the stitches out, I could go back to the Princess Royal. Valerie and Doris came up to take me back by car to Balcombe Ward. After about three days the stitches were taken out and I was able to go home. I cannot speak highly enough of how kind and helpful the staff were to me during my many stays in Balcombe Ward, and I also owe a lot to Dr Metcalfe and Dr Harding, my GP. It was a few months after I had my bypass and new valves that I had a permanent pacemaker fitted at the hospital in Brighton.

Early in 1995, as I belong to the 'Friends of The Museum' at Bovington, I received six invitation tickets to the 50th anniversary VE Day celebrations to be held at Weymouth, which is only about 20 miles from Bovington. It was hoped to be the largest street party ever held, stretching for one mile along the promenade. Valerie and Gordon have a very large trailer tent, and it was decided to book it in at a caravan site just at the back of the tank training grounds at Bovington and the four of us were to stay in the trailer that weekend. We have two very good friends in our wine club, John and Jill Boxall, who I invited to come with the other two tickets. They were pleased to accept and bring their caravan along. During the stay we would be able to visit the Museum, although I have been many times, I find it very enjoyable. As my son Dennis lives in Plymouth, I never pass that way without calling in. As I said earlier, when I was doing my training, it had become my second home.

We arrived on a Friday, and went over to the Museum on the Saturday and later visited other places of interest. The celebrations were being held the next day. John and Jill had their caravan next to the trailer tent. It was very early on the Sunday morning that John was banging the door of our trailer tent. He had the radio on in their caravan and had just heard the news that the 1500 tables and chairs which were due to arrive at Wool station on the Saturday evening had gone missing. The radio was putting out calls for help. We had already decided to go into Weymouth early to park the cars and we arrived at 9 o'clock, although the celebrations were not due to start until 10 o'clock. Lorries were arriving with hundreds of chairs and tables. I understand that large firms with furniture and hotels and others had joined in. Fortunately, it was going to be a very hot day. Gordon and John were helping to unload lorries which were queued up, waiting to move down the mile-long prom. I saw one lorry with new tables and chairs still with their protective paper on.

The whole mile was split into zones, so everyone arriving had a zone number on their tickets. Doris, Jill and myself were helping with paper tablecloths. The celebrations started one hour late. It certainly was a wonderful day. It seemed it would be a disaster for the organisers in the first place, but one could see the old war spirit had come back in that morning, with everyone helping each other. I have a video of the Weymouth celebrations. This was the first time I had gone back to Weymouth since we sailed from there to France. On the Monday was a parade along the prom, in which some tanks from Bovington took part. The one thing I would have liked to do would be to ride in a tank round the training grounds. I did ask a few years ago when I was at Bovington, but was told this would not be possible as it was military and the insurance would not cover a civilian. I am not joining up again just for a ride! As I am coming up to 82, I would need a fork-lift truck to get me into the tank, but I am sure I would enjoy it more than flying in Concorde.

15

Appreciation

I was now wondering what I could do to raise some money for the British Heart Foundation to show my appreciation for all that had been done for me, and something to help others. I was sitting on our lawn assembling switches when a light aircraft came over. It had, I am sure, come up from Shoreham, which has an airfield where one can learn to fly or take pleasure trips. I had not taken the controls of a light plane since my lessons at Biggin Hill, but felt this would be a good idea to raise some money for the BHF. At that time many people said that when anyone had a bypass or new valve for the heart that it was not wise to fly again. I went to Dr Harding to ask his opinion about flying. His answer was that I could do whatever I wished, as I was just as fit now as I was before the trouble. I phoned Shoreham and told them what I would like to do. Even they felt a little apprehensive about me wanting to do this so soon after the operation.

When I told them I had seen my doctor and he had given me the all clear, they suggested I should go down and take a lesson flight, which would be at a reduced charge. This I did and found that although the controls were still very much the same, there was much more comfort than the last time I had flown, 22 years before. I now set the wheels in motion for sponsorship. I contacted our local paper, the *Mid-Sussex Times*, and they gave a very good write-up. The *Evening Argus* contacted me, and they also gave me some editorial space. Through this publicity, sponsor money started to come in. Radio Mercury came to the house, and I carried out a short recording which went out on the air one evening.

I booked the flight for my birthday, 15 December 1992. This would be seven months after the operation. The plane I would be flying was a Piper Warrior so I could take two passengers. The weather was very good on the day of the flight. Valerie and Richard came as passengers, Richard armed with his camera. The pilot took off and, once we were airborne, handed the controls over to me. I went out over Chichester first, as two members of our wine club, Sid and Rita Nieve, would be there that day and had sponsored me. After doing two circuits over the town, I headed back over the South Downs towards Haywards Heath, coming in over the Princess Royal Hospital. I then came directly over our house. Doris and the others were in the back garden. I circled twice over Haywards Heath and then headed back to Shoreham. At our next wine meeting in January 1993, I was able to present to a representative of the British Heart Foundation, a cheque close on £1,000. In a write-up later by the *Mid-Sussex Times*, the heading was 'Fred Flies By To Say Thanks'. I just wanted to prove that so shortly after a bypass you can do what you want. A lot of people get very apprehensive, but I wanted to show them not to be so.

I went in to the Sussex Eye Hospital and had my first cataract operation. This was a great success, but I would have to wait for another year or so before I could have the other eye operated on.

It was now possible to fly into Belfast City airport, transfer to a small plane and fly up to Londonderry. This was a lot more convenient as this airport was only about ten miles from Strabane. The first time I flew into Derry airport I noticed there was a private flying club at the airport. During my stay, I contacted this club about making flights, and they said that I would be very welcome, and also, I was pleased to hear, that they had a Piper Warrior. I had several flights in this plane and now know many of the pilots and members. I took Bridget and Jennifer up to the club, with a view to taking them up for a flight. Steve, a pilot who I go up with, came in to say there was a very high wind and said it would not be very comfortable being blown all over the skies. There was a chap in the club room who remarked that I looked disappointed. I said it was disappointing for Bridget and Jennifer, who had not been up in a light aircraft before. I remarked that when learning to fly at Biggin Hill, I had become used to being disappointed because of the weather changing so often. He then introduced himself as Tom, who had also learnt to fly at Biggin Hill. He told me he had his own plane at the club and was an aerobatics pilot, and he asked if I would like to go up with him the next time I was there. One evening, when Tom came in he offered to take me up. He took me out over that area and carried out a few stunts. It was a very exciting flight. Each time I go over, if the weather is acceptable, I always take a flight. Although I have travelled the whole of Donegal by car many times, it really is out of this world to fly a light plane over the mountains there.

We were invited to a wedding in Haywards Heath. The service was held at St Wilfrids Church at 2 a.m., and Doris and myself were making our way out of the church when I stopped before going out of the main doors to let people pass me who wanted to get outside for photographs. I went to go forward, not realising I had stopped on the edge of a small step. I fell forward, flat on my face with my arms out in front and onto the stone floor. I got up with a terrible pain in my left arm. Valerie was sure I had broken my arm. Doris's brother, Les, who was there, kindly took me up to the hospital. Les left me there when we realised it was going to take a long wait. He went back to the reception, which was being held in the United Services Club. After X-rays it was confirmed that I had broken my arm just above the wrist. As the hand appeared to be hanging on one side it was decided to give me a local anaesthetic to try to manipulate it back in place, but because I had had a small snack before leaving for the wedding, I would have to wait until later that evening before this could be done. This was carried out, but not successfully.

I came home and within a few days went to see a surgeon, who told me he would have to put a plate in my arm to keep the hand in its right position. I was admitted to have this carried out. The anaesthetist came to see me about an hour before the operation. She told me she had a problem as she could not give me a general anaesthetic because of my heart. She would give me a local, which would only last one hour, and she felt sure the operation would take longer than that. I said as I was in her hands, I would have to put up with it.

When I arrived to have the anaesthetic, they started by giving me a shock treatment to deaden the left arm. They put a probe in the palm of my hand and another behind my left ear. Each time they gave me a shock, I pleaded for them to stop. They were putting pins in my arm to see how dead it was. After a while, I was taken into the operating theatre. The surgeon nodded to me and at the same time cut my arm open. I told him that he had just cut my arm open, admittedly it was not very painful, but I knew he had done it and then I passed out. I woke in a ward, and Doris was sitting by the bed. I learnt later that I had been given a general anaesthetic. I had to go back to have the plaster off and a sleeve fitted, and when I saw the surgeon, I told him I was very annoyed with the shock treatment. He said he was very surprised when they took me in, that I was still awake. I knew it was not his fault and everything was being done for my own good. If they had explained to me about the treatment I would have been happy to go along with it. When something like this is inflicted without prior warning it really is a shock.

Over the next two years we went over to Ireland for our usual visits. Michael had completed the bungalow, and we stayed with them. Michael is a caretaker at a school about four miles from the bungalow. When we stayed there, I took Michael to work in the mornings and he kindly let me have the use of the car through the day, and I would go back to pick him up in the evening.

16

Clippers

A new restaurant opened in Strabane called the Mill Inn. It is owned by a young and very pleasant chap called Michael Brown. We always make a point to visit a couple of times when we are over. We always go over to the south and visit Mrs Quinn, who now lives on her own; the family are all grown up and married with children. Bill and Austin, two of the sons, live nearby so she always has company. Mike O'Hanlon had now retired and lives with his wife, Margaret, in a small village in Donegal called Ballindrait. They have a very unusual garden with trees, shrubs and tropical plants. They have also designed it with small paths going up and own. You do not walk very far from the back of the house before you feel lost in another world. At the back of the garden is a river, the Deele, which is a tributary of the river Foyle, which flows in through Londonderry from Lough Foyle. Mike, or Nutty Mike, as he was called in England, has a canoe and often takes a trip on the river. He loves to play the piano and sings away when he has company. He is still a terrific entertainer. Mike told me a lot about the Clipper Carltons. He used to drive the bus in Ireland as they travelled around doing their shows. He was the only one who did not drink or smoke as the rest of the showband did. After the shows he would have to wait around for them, and very often did not get home until the next morning. I would have loved to have seen the Clippers.

Sadie from Philadelphia was telling me that the Clippers came to Philadelphia and she and Jerry went to see them. Sadie invited them up to the house for a meal. Mike and Terry both lived in Strabane. Terry was in the band and Sadie knew them. Mike was surprised when we told him we had stayed with Sadie and Jerry several times. Michael phoned us with some good news. There had been a banquet in Omagh, which is also in Tyrone, in honour of the Clipper Carltons. Someone at the banquet had persuaded them to make a two-year comeback with an open cheque to set them up. When I saw Mike he told me he had agreed to drive the bus, providing the others would not hang around drinking after the shows. Michael had got us tickets for a show at Bundoran, which is a seaside town in Donegal. We went over and decided to go out there in the afternoon, have tea and go to the hotel in the evening for the show. When we arrived, the weather was very bad. We had an early tea and got to the hotel very early. Doris, Bridget, Michael and myself went in to have a steady quiet drink until the Clippers' show. We went into the hall at 10 o'clock, expecting the Clippers' show to start. There was another showband on, which was very good. In fact the Clippers never came on until midnight and went on until about 4 a.m. It was daylight by the time we got back home. It was a show well worth waiting to see and hear.

We were over again when the Clippers were doing a show at the Fir Trees Hotel in Strabane. This time we went to the hotel for an evening meal and later to see the show again. It was soon after this that Mike asked me if I would like to go down to Castlebar with the band for a show they were going to do, and it was being televised. This was on a Sunday, and I had booked with my flying club to take some friends for a flight. I was very disappointed that I had to turn down Mike's invitation, but could not let my friends down. However, Margaret taped the show for me, which I still have. They toured for eighteen months and then gave up. I believe there are now only two of the original nine left alive.

I decided to take a balloon flight. I tried very hard to persuade Doris to come with me; I am sure she would have enjoyed it once we were up, but she declined by saying 'You won't get me up in one of those bloody things!' I booked up to take the flight on a Sunday morning from Midhurst. It was an early flight, and I had to go to a hotel car park at 8 a.m. This meant leaving home about 6.30 a.m. It was a morning with a very heavy frost – ideal for a flight. I met the organisers, and there were seven of us going up, plus the pilot. We set off in a minibus, with the wagon carrying the balloon, basket and the necessary gear. We went to a field and laid out the balloon on the ground, each passenger was given a job to do in preparing the balloon. We were very pleased to do this.

When the balloon was ready, there was a slight hold-up as another passenger wished to go on our flight. This made eight in the basket, which was a bit tight. However, we took off. It was a perfect morning, the air was clear but the only trouble was that at 500 feet we ran out of wind. We rose another 500 feet and then drifted along out over Petworth. I was surprised how many deer there were in the park. We landed in a ploughed field; the flight had taken one hour from the time we left. The white pick-up vehicles had been following the balloon, and as soon as we landed the vehicles were there. Now, because the balloon had not landed on this farmer's land before and they had not received any permission for it to land, we were not allowed to get out of the basket until the farmer had been found to get permission. The truck brought the farmer and his wife back, and bottles of champagne were opened and everyone joined in. It is perhaps the only time that I would be drinking champagne at 10 o'clock on a very cold frosty Sunday morning in the middle of a ploughed field.

17

The Latest Battle

For some time now my head wound had been getting much worse and I had to go to see Dr Harding. It was very inflamed and tender. He prescribed stronger painkillers, of which I could take up to eight a day. He suggested that I should get on to the War Pensions Department at Blackpool and ask for a deterioration increase regarding my head wound. He was very surprised when I told him that my War Disabled Pension did not include anything for my head wound. He advised me to notify them straight away.

I wrote on 29 February 1996, explaining that the pain had become considerably worse over recent years and my doctor had said it was a form of neuralgia from the head wound. I received an acknowledgement that they had received my letter and I filled in the claim forms on 29 March. It was in April when I was advised by the War Pensions Agency that a Mrs Horwood would be calling to see me. When she came she assured me she knew nothing about my claim, her job as Welfare Officer was to visit all war disabled pensioners in the Sussex area in alphabetical order, and it so happened she was now visiting all the 'G's. She assured me I should have no problems with my claim, but to call on her if I did.

Dr Harding had arranged for me to have X-rays on my head in case any shrapnel was still there. I was X-rayed from the waist upwards. The head was clear, but three pieces appeared on my chest. These had not been there on previous X-rays and I had also had X-rays when I complained about pains in my head in 1987. It was arranged for a doctor, on behalf of the War Pensions Agency, to come in July to my house for a medical examination. This was a Dr Valli-Jones from Burgess Hill. After he had examined me I asked him why he had not looked at my head wound or asked me anything about it. He assured me he knew all about it and he would get his report in straight away. He also said I would have no trouble with my claim. I knew Dr Harding had also sent in a medical report. I was now confident that this would soon be settled with the reports all in my favour. Doris was always convinced my claim would be turned down, and when I asked why she said it was because I had the wrong name!

It was now coming up to our Golden wedding anniversary, 8 June 1996. Valerie, Raymond and Richard arranged a reception at the St Francis Club. Dennis would be coming up from Plymouth with his family. Doris and I particularly requested donations to the British Heart Foundation, rather than presents. I also arranged to fly a plane over the town the same morning for sponsor money, again for the BHF. We had a sit-down meal for 136, and after the meal Richard gave a speech, followed by Paddy Henry who, as I have said before, is a great friend of the family. After this first-class anniversary reception we flew over to Ireland, where we were given another reception at the All Stars Club in Strabane. That morning I carried out another sponsored flight from the flying club, over Strabane. £515 was collected in lieu of presents and £195 in sponsorship, a grand total of £710, which we passed on the BHF. We also did receive presents from the family and close friends.

It was November 1996 when I received a letter from the War Pensions in Blackpool to say my claim had been turned down. I could not believe this with all the medical evidence in my favour. Also in their letter, they said they would write to me in November 2000, when they would review my assessment. As I was then turned 80, this really was a laugh. I then approached the British Legion, of which I am a member, for their help. Their Service Secretary came to see me. His name was Harry Winn, and he was very helpful. Harry wrote to his head office in a very helpful letter explaining my case, and he also asked

181

for a complete review of my disabilities. In a letter from Harry's head office for the British Legion, they stated that I may have the right to appeal.

It was in March 1997 that my battle with the War Pensions Agency started again. From the letters I was receiving, it was obvious we were back to square one and I would be going through the same procedures as I had started in the previous year because of the request for a complete review. I cannot speak highly enough of Harry Winn for his interest in my case. I decided to approach Paddy Henry to see if he could help. Paddy was more than happy to take on the bureaucrats!

Medical reports were obtained, including another visit from Dr Valli-Jones, who showed me his report and another from Dr Harding. We even obtained a report from Vic Haydon, my hairdresser, who had now retired. Because the Agency was still not responding to my claim but only carrying out delaying tactics, such as sending acknowledgement, but no further action being taken, Paddy made an appointment with our MP, Nicholas Soames. We went to see him on 30 June 1997, and the only letter he kept was the one Paddy had prepared for me setting out the history of my head wound. I felt when talking to him that, although he did not say anything, he felt that the pension of 30 per cent which I had been receiving over all the past years was not adequate. On 8 July my pension was increased to 80 per cent for pain and stiffness in both knees and tinnitus. They also said that it was accepted that the shrapnel wound to the head in 1941 was caused by war service, but that they considered I had no remaining disablement from this injury and no increase in my pension would be given for this. It was now obvious that this would have to be decided in the appeal court. It was beyond Paddy's understanding that with the Agency's own medical reports in my favour, they could still say that there was no remaining disablement. I asked Paddy if he would represent me, and, as he enjoys a good fight, he agreed.

I made an appointment to see a consultant neurologist, Mr Peter J. Ward, and Paddy came along with all the accumulated paperwork. Mr Ward saw me on my own, and after taking notes on the history of the wound made his own report without refer-

182

ence to the previous reports.. Further delaying tactics from the Agency and many letters from Paddy eventually resulted in another 10 per cent pension for my neuralgia. This had been Dr Harding's diagnosis all of two years previously.

I feel it is a shame that an 81-year-old veteran should have been put through all this bureaucracy. Dr Harding told me that it is with age that old wounds flare up. I cannot understand, in my case, with two medical reports from my own GP, two medical reports from the agency's own doctor and a report from the hairdresser, that someone sitting in an office in Blackpool can say he is not prepared to believe these reports, and only after a final consultant's report, which I had to obtain myself, was a satisfactory result obtained.

My sincere thanks to Dr Harding, Paddy Henry, Hon. Nicholas Soames, Margaret Horwood, Harry Winn, Linda Helliwell and Vic Haydon for bringing this episode to a successful conclusion.

Early in December 1996 , Doris became ill and was admitted to Balcombe Ward at the Princess Royal. She was discharged after one week, but in the next two weeks she was readmitted and then discharged again. She was home for Christmas, but I was worried as she appeared still to be very unwell. On Sunday, 4 January 1997, she became very ill and I contacted Dr Harding, who immediately had her taken back into hospital, but this time into Pyecombe Ward. On Wednesday, 7 January, I left her just after visiting hours at 8 p.m. She was sitting in a chair by the side of the bed. She did not walk with me to the door of the ward as she usually did, because she felt very tired.

It was 1.30 a.m. that night that the hospital rang to ask me to go up. They said Doris had collapsed and was transferred to Balcombe Ward, and to call the family to go up as well. I phoned them and we went to the hospital. Dennis had left Plymouth and would arrive at the hospital by early morning. Dr Metcalfe had Doris in the operating theatre, putting in a temporary pacemaker. When she arrived back in the ward I went in to see her. She wanted to sleep, so I left her for a while.

At 12.20 p.m. on 8 January 1997, Doris passed away. After 50 years of being married, it was a terrible blow to me. She had

183

been a magnificent wife and mother. We had her cremated and her ashes buried in the garden of remembrance at the Western Road Cemetery, which is just round the corner from my house. I am very fortunate in the fact that I have Richard and Gillian living next door and Raymond and Heather just round the corner from me. Valerie and Gordon are only two miles away. Dennis and Sylvia are the farthest away, in Plymouth, but they visit often with their two sons. Also, with the business operating from the back of the house with its offices and stores there is always company to talk to, and I will always have my friends in Ireland to visit.

18

Going On

Early in November 1996, a small black-and-white kitten wandered into the house on a Sunday afternoon. Doris never liked cats, as they were always messing in her flower garden, and ordered me to throw it out. On the Monday morning the wind was blowing and it was raining hard. I opened the garage and found the kitten sleeping so I brought it indoors and, when Doris got up, it was sleeping on my lap. That morning I tried to find out who it belonged to, but without success, so Paws and Claws took it to the cats' home in Burgess Hill. They would keep it for three weeks and, if unclaimed, it would be put to sleep. They said they would phone to let me know what was to happen. The time was up on a Friday morning, and Doris asked me to phone them. Doris had changed her mind and said we would have it. We signed the papers to adopt it. We were told it was a she cat, and called it Bubbles, but when I took it to the vet's it turned out to be a tom, but we kept the name Bubbles anyway. Bubbles settled in very well, and Doris became very fond of him. Since her death, Bubbles has filled a space in my life and is a reminder of our last months together.

While I was away in Ireland in March 1998, I received a phone call from Raymond on a Saturday afternoon to say he had married Heather Upton at the Registry Office in Haywards Heath. This came as a surprise to me, as earlier that week Heather had taken me to the airport and had not mentioned one word of their intentions. I wished them the best of luck, and that evening took Bridget, Michael, Noel and Jennifer to the Mill

185

House restaurant for a meal and a drink to Raymond and Heather's marriage. Michael provided a bottle of the best wine from his cellar (at the usual price, of course!).

On the evening of 31 July 1998, Richard and myself took a balloon flight from Hickstead out over Burgess Hill, with a very good view of Haywards Heath. We eventually had a very dramatic landing in the grounds of the Buxted Manor Hotel after the basket, in which there were 13 of us, hit the top of a tree with some considerable force. All was well, and we all enjoyed the pleasure of a champagne celebration drink. I enjoyed this flight more than my previous flight, as I could look down on a countryside which I knew very well.

During my visits back to Bovington Tank Museum, I took photographs showing the hard road built along the side of the dirt track. This must be a great advantage over when we trained during the winter of 1938–39. The tanks were in a terrible state after a couple of miles on the training ground.

On 5 September 1998, I went to Ireland for a wedding and met Sadie and her now-married four sons. As I was going over to America, Sadie invited me to visit them in Philadelphia. My next trip to America was on Concorde to New York. My first flight was when I was 13 in 1929 – and what a contrast. Flying at 60,000 feet, with a speed up to 1350 mph and with an outside temperature of –60 degrees C, the flight took 3 hours and 15 minutes. I took the usual tours of New York, a helicopter flight over the city and a cruise round Manhattan, plus an evening on Broadway to see *The Phantom of the Opera*. I then travelled down to Philadelphia by Amtrak, staying with Sadie and Jerry for two days, then back up to New York and home on a jumbo jet.

I have always wanted to take on gliding, and as there is a gliding club at Ringmer, which is only about half an hour by car, I have been in contact with them and am waiting for a day when the weather is ideal for me to take my first lesson. As I do not have to book in advance, this is an advantage over having to book when flying a light aircraft.

A final update on my family: Valerie and Gordon live in Lindfield. Valerie is still a nursing sister at the Princess Royal Hospital, and Gordon is a postman.

Raymond and Heather live round the corner, and Raymond is the older partner in the business and Heather is a dental receptionist.

Dennis and his wife Sylvia live in Portsmouth. Dennis completed 25 years in the Navy and is now with the police force. Sylvia is a hairdresser. They have three sons.

Richard and his wife Gillian live next door. Richard is the other partner in the family business. He serves as a Councillor for Haywards Heath Town and District councils, and he is a Justice of the Peace. They have a son, Robert, who was born prematurely but is now progressing very well.

The business continues to expand. We have a staff of 12, with 10 vehicles on the road.

Since starting this book I have set myself targets to do things I have always wanted to do. I have flown in Concorde, nipped through the Channel Tunnel and am planning a Rhine cruise as well as the gliding lessons, and I fully intend to be around to celebrate the Millennium in good style.